A GUIDE TO SELECTING AND USING BIBLE COMMENTARIES

Douglas Stuart

WORD PUBLISHING
Dallas · London · Sydney · Singapore

A Guide to Selecting and Using Bible Commentaries

Library of Congress Cataloging-in-Publication Data

Stuart, Douglas
    A guide to selecting and using Bible commentaries / Douglas Stuart.
        p.   cm.
    Includes bibliographical references.
    ISBN 0-8499-3228-9
    1. Bible—Commentaries—History and criticism.   2. Bible—Commentaries—Bibliography.   3. Bibliography—Best books—Bible.
I. Title.
BS491.2.S78   1990
220.7—dc20   90-41238
                                                                        CIP

Printed in the United States of America
0 1 2 3 9 BKC 9 8 7 6 5 4 3 2 1

To
Milliesha Sarah,
Delia Esther,
Raul Jonathan

Contents

Preface

Not every book that contains comments on the Bible is a commentary. Bible handbooks, for example, usually have in them both outlines and summaries of the contents of the sixty-six Bible books. But they are not considered commentaries. The longer Bible dictionaries and encyclopedias also contain outlines and content summaries of the various Bible books, but they are not commentaries, either. Study Bibles typically include brief comments on each passage and brief introductions to the individual books of the Bible but the term *commentary* is not applied to them. Moreover, books that analyze selected aspects of a biblical book or books, even in great detail (e.g., books with titles like Studies in . . . or Paul's View of . . .) are also not commentaries in the sense that the term commentary is normally used.

Basic Definition of Commentary

So what makes a book a commentary? Simply, *a commentary is a book written to provide a relatively full explanation of the meaning of the passages in a portion of the Bible.* There are four things that make this happen:

1. Length. It has to be long enough to provide a "relatively full explanation" of the passages it comments on or it isn't a commentary in the normal sense. Obviously, some commentaries are more complete than others.

2. Depth. It has to go into enough detail and discuss problems or difficult wordings carefully enough, or it won't succeed in

making the meaning clear to the reader. Obviously, some commentaries fail to perform this task adequately and some are more thorough than others.

3. Organization. It has to be organized in a manner that makes it possible for the reader to locate the comments on the passage(s) he or she is interested in understanding. In almost all instances this means that the commentary has to array its comments in the same order as the biblical passages. A commentary, in other words, is a reference book, and ability to get speedily at its information is important.

4. Attention to the text. It has to pay attention relentlessly to the words of Scripture themselves. Some books that call themselves commentaries are actually centered around illustrations or other ideas that are essentially nothing more than the writer's views on the topics under consideration. The Bible raises the topics, and the "commentator" gives you his or her opinions on those topics. A true commentary is, however, interested in what the Bible says, not what some modern person thinks about the same topics. Is the author carefully explaining what the passage means? If not, no matter how interesting the book may be, it's not really a commentary.

Note: Don't fail to catch the importance of the word *passages* in the basic definition above. In the first chapter of this book the significance of that word will be described much more fully.

Of course, no commentary can do everything. They all have their limitations, flaws, biases, and omissions. They all differ in quality. They are inconsistent—brilliant in one place, dismal in another. They differ in theological orientation, in scope, in format, in technical precision, and in clarity. But then, that's why you're reading a book like this—to get some guidance on choosing among all the types.

This Book Is Selective

Over the years, around the world, thousands of commentaries have been published. There have been so many that even huge multi-volume bibliographic guides to publications in biblical studies don't list all of them. It would probably be the work of a lifetime to compile a truly complete list, and even then the list would keep getting longer by hundreds of titles every year. But that doesn't mean we can't give you some helpful advice about choosing commentaries, as well as a commentary list that will do you a lot of good, as long as we place reasonable limits on the size of our list. Let's consider those limits.

1. English.

First, we will limit our consideration of commentaries to those that are written in English. Scholars would not be justified in limiting themselves in this way, of course, but scholars are already aware of their need to read a variety of foreign languages. Most readers of this book cannot read (at least not well) the languages that most of the world's existing non-English commentaries are published in: Latin, German, French, Italian, Dutch, Hebrew, Spanish, Norwegian, Swedish, Greek, Portuguese, Czech, Finnish, Japanese, and Russian, to name the main ones. Fortunately, English is such a predominant language in our world, and biblical scholarship is so common to English-speaking cultures that most significant information necessary to understanding the Bible can be located in English. However, the commentary format has actually been employed by German-speaking scholars far more frequently than by English-speaking scholars, and there have been, accordingly, at least twice as many commentaries published in the last hundred years in German as in English (in the case of some biblical books, four or five times as many!). The German commentaries are not necessarily better, however. The German higher education system rewards sheer quantity of publication above all other considerations in the granting of promotions, and the predictable result is a steady flood of commentaries and other publications, only some of which are worth using.

2. In print or widely available in libraries.

Second, we will limit our consideration of commentaries to those that are currently in print and those that once were considered important enough to have been purchased commonly by libraries. We live in an age in which books go out of print rapidly, since publishers cannot afford the storage costs for books that are not selling briskly. To recommend books that you could get only at a major or specialized library, or through a rare book dealer, would probably not be very helpful, so what we'll recommend will be books that we believe are likely to be reasonably available to you at present.

3. Sold or available in the U. S./Canada.

Third, we will limit our consideration of commentaries to those that are for sale, or held widely in libraries, in the United States and Canada, where most of the readers of this book will live. English-language commentaries primarily available in places like the British Isles, India, or South Africa will be excluded.

4. Modern.

The commentaries of the church fathers, of medieval scholars, of the Reformers, and of others prior to this century contain insights and perspectives that might be of value to any reader. Nevertheless, so much has been learned recently in the fields of biblical languages, the literature of the biblical era, archaeology, and other areas that modern commentators are aware of, that virtually all older commentaries must be considered dated. Thus, even though we know that there is much to be learned from the commentaries of such fine scholars as Martin Luther or John Wesley, we limit our coverage in this volume to commentaries written during or just before the twentieth century. Only such commentaries can reflect awareness of new discoveries, and it is our judgment that most readers will prefer commentaries that are up-to-date in that way.

5. Nonspecialized.

We also cannot include highly specialized commentaries. For instance, homiletical commentaries are designed to provide preachers with illustrations and arguments in support of the text, but not straightforward explanations of the text. Thus, such series as the Knox Preaching Guides (Louisville: Westminster/John Knox) or the Communicator's Commentary (Dallas: Word Books) or the Proclamation Commentaries (Philadelphia: Fortress) are not included here. They have interest for preachers, but not as commentaries per se. Likewise, archaeological commentaries (designed to focus on archaeological evidence relating to parts of the various biblical books) and series that concentrate on one aspect of interpretation, like commentaries only on literary forms (including the Forms of Old Testament Literature series published by Eerdmans), will also not be given consideration in this book. All these have their place, but not in a book surveying "commentaries" as people normally understand them.

6. Not omitted by accident.

We are also bound to miss some good commentaries. This won't be intentional, but it's bound to happen that some perfectly fine commentaries will not have come to our attention for one reason or another, or perhaps we will have assumed them to be still out of print when they had in fact been republished (publishers often don't give advance notice of such things), or for any number of other reasons.

7. Worth listing.

Finally, we are going to exclude many commentaries intentionally. When we think a commentary is unreliable, or seriously deficient in coverage of the portion of Scripture it covers, or of low quality, or just not worth listing for whatever reason, it won't be included here. This decision is based on our best sense of the readership of this book. We want to give you a listing of the commentaries that you might conceivably buy and use, not those you wouldn't want to have anything to do with anyway. Naturally, our decisions on what to include and what to exclude will be subjective, but there's no alternative. We can't mention everything, we can't list every book we *don't* recommend, and there's no value in making our decisions on a merely mechanistic basis (e.g., including every commentary in a series when some of that series' commentaries are just plain awful). If we hurt the feelings of some commentary writers by doing this, we can only say that that isn't our purpose at all. We are simply aiming to list what we think our readers need and want most, and what we can justify as being *worth listing*, even if far from perfect.

1

What Commentaries Are and Are Not

Basic Orientation

Commentaries are books that provide passage-by-passage explanations of books in the Bible. There are, of course, commentaries on other kinds of books (e.g., on Shakespeare's plays or Homer's *Iliad*) but the vast majority of commentaries are written to explain biblical books, and the word *commentary* is used nearly always in reference to the area of biblical studies.

Occasionally, a single commentary may cover only part of a biblical book, but that is not common. Some commentaries are very brief—shorter than the biblical books they explain. Obviously, these commentaries are too short to comment on each verse, or even to provide more than a simple summary of the passages in the book or books they cover. Other commentaries are so detailed that they can devote, if necessary, thousands of words of analysis to a single Bible verse. You have to want to know an awful lot about that verse to read ten or fifteen pages on it. But when that is what you want, nothing less than a very detailed commentary will do.

The idea of explaining Bible books by means of commentaries is not new. The earliest written commentaries that still exist come from the Dead Sea Scrolls (around the time of Christ), but as early as 443 B.C. Ezra's aides gave oral commentaries to the crowds in Jerusalem seeking to understand the Pentateuch (Nehemiah 8:7–8). The popularity of commentaries, however, has never been greater than it is today. The last couple of centuries have been the heyday of commentaries, and at the present time more commentaries are being written than ever before.

Commentaries and Passages

Almost all commentaries analyze passages—the literary units that, all together, make up books of the Bible. If it doesn't go passage by passage through a book of the Bible, it isn't a commentary in the usual sense. If a book summarizes the content of several chapters at a time (as some Bible handbooks do, for example), it may be a synopsis or a survey outline, but not really a commentary. If a book analyzes only the individual verses of a biblical book in isolation from one another, without reference to how those verses contribute to the sense of the passages they are part of, it isn't a typical commentary either. (I don't know of any commentaries that actually analyze verses without reference to their contribution to passages, but if one were written, I don't think many people would buy it.) Many commentaries are detailed enough to be able to say something about every verse in the book they are written on, but you will notice that they do so with a concern to fit each verse within its passage, not merely to see what it says independently within itself.

Passages vs. Chapters and Verses

Passages are very important to commentaries. Chapters and verses are not. Chapters and verses are helpful divisions made to the text of the Bible so that people can quickly and conveniently find a particular portion of text. But chapters and verse divisions were not made all that carefully in the first place, and therefore readers should not pay a lot of attention to them. They do help you find your place, but they don't help you understand what it says once you've found it. At first, chapter numbers, and then later verse numbers, were added to the biblical text during the Middle Ages, long after all of the Bible was written, and with a great deal of disregard for the fact that some passages are very short and others are very long. Thus some chapters in the Bible group together several individual passages, while others contain only part of a passage. In the latter cases, the chapter divisions actually interrupt the flow of a passage if you pay attention to them. Therefore, writers of commentaries try not to pay much attention to chapter and verse divisions, precisely because they do not want to miss the logic of the self-contained building blocks of text (the passages).

The Importance of Passages

Correctly identifying passages is a very important part of almost any nonhaphazard use you might make of the Bible. If you're reading through a biblical book, being aware of the changing passages helps you be aware of the subject matter. You move from one passage to another as you move from one topic to another. You can always tell when the passage is changing by the fact that the topic is changing (and vice versa). It can happen that several passages are devoted to the same overall topic, but if so, the passages will be distinguishable from one another by the fact that they deal with different *sub*-topics under the same general topic.

Commentators (the authors of commentaries) are not going to worry much about where the chapter or verse numbers may appear in the biblical book their commentary is written to explain. They are going to concentrate on passages. Naturally, if the length of the commentary they are writing allows them to make comments about individual verses within passages, they will do so. But they'll feel very free to group two or more verses together and discuss them as one unit, and they'll also feel free to discuss only part of a single verse as a unit. And whatever else they may say about the verses, if they are proper commentators they will be sure to say how each verse—or part of a verse, or group of verses—contributes to the meaning of the passage they are writing about.

Why Do We Need Commentaries at All?

The basic reason there are commentaries is that everybody can use help understanding the Bible. There are two reasons for this. Both reasons are really very simple, but they are important to understand: (1) *All parts of the Bible are not equally comprehensible.* (2) *Not all people are equally able to figure out the meaning of any given part.* If you already know that, fine. But a great many people either don't know it or don't want to admit it. They believe that the Holy Spirit ought to make everything in the Bible plain to any believer who reads it sincerely, without other aids being necessary. This is a widely held belief, and if it were true, there would hardly be any need for commentaries. But the Bible itself never says any such thing. In fact, a good commentary is exactly the sort of thing that might help people understand more accurately those passages (e.g., John 14:26) that they *think* teach that the meaning of everything in the Bible ought to be plain to any devoted reader.

That is, any commentary on the Gospel of John worth its price should help the reader realize that (1) Jesus' promises to his apostles were not necessarily promises to all believers, and (2) he did not promise even his apostles that they would automatically be experts on all of Scripture. Further, any reliable commentary on any New Testament passage dealing with "teaching" should help the reader understand that some people are gifted by God as teachers precisely because other people need to be taught what the Bible means. In other words, God understands and has planned for the fact that everybody can use some help in understanding the Bible—and some more than others.

Commentaries and the Priesthood of All Believers

At this point you might, quite rightly, be wondering: What about Martin Luther's famous affirmation of "the priesthood of all believers"? Isn't it basic to biblical Christianity that we should never let someone else tell us what the Bible says? Not at all. Martin Luther did not say that we should have a "priesthood of *each* believer." He never implied that *each* person is his or her own priest, interpreting the Bible in splendid isolation, ignorant of what others have studied hard to learn. He said "*all* believers" and those who know his writings know that he considered all believers *together*, acting as a group, to be the authoritative interpreters of the Word of God with the aid of the Holy Spirit (rather than the pope or his aides in Rome). Differing gifts combine to provide for the citizens of God's kingdom an understanding that they can all benefit from. The people who write commentaries can contribute a great deal to the understanding of the Bible for the benefit of all Christians. It is the task of the church, as a group, to learn and guard the truth.

Luther, a prolific commentary writer himself, was hardly against the idea of people sharing their learning via commentaries. What he wanted to protect was the truth for all believers. His concern was to challenge the elitist notion that only one individual or a small group of clergy were authorized to recognize and declare the meaning of the Scriptures. Luther attacked the concept that the mediators (clergy) should control the message. The whole church, working together, not individuals doing their own thing, should serve the Lord as his priests, guarding the truth of his word, as Exodus 19:6 implies.

Are All Commentaries Equally Trustworthy, Then?

Heavens, no. Some are terrible, written by people who didn't know enough about the book they were writing on to do a creditable job. Others are so hostile to the accuracy of the Bible that they spend most of their time reconstructing the text (in some cases rewriting it) according to a skeptical view of the Bible. Such books are really not commentaries on the Bible as much as they are commentaries on some skeptical scholar's view of those parts of the Bible that he or she decided might be original. Other commentaries are well-intentioned but erratic, covering some passages brilliantly, other passages sloppily. Still others are so distorted by theological bias that they keep from the readers the most likely meaning and try to foist off on them the narrow point of view of the commentator as if there were no other.

The Worst Kind of Commentary

But perhaps the worst kind of commentary of all is the commentary that contains little or no data, i.e., is composed almost entirely of statements of opinion that are not supported by citation of facts. Even a commentary authored by an avowed skeptic can be used profitably, if you're very careful to sort out the facts from the opinion and let the facts help you understand the passage you're studying. But a data-free commentary is nothing but opinion. You have no way of knowing whether its opinions are right or wrong unless you have some data by which to evaluate them. No commentator is so trustworthy that he or she should be allowed to tell you what to think about a passage without explaining to you what his or her reasons are—that is, what evidence he or she has for the opinions offered in the commentary. There's nothing wrong with opinion. But opinion alone is almost worthless to you if it is not accompanied by good reasoning based upon factual information. Always demand that your commentary show you the facts. Whenever it doesn't, you should accept its conclusions only with the greatest caution. We'll say much more about how to evaluate a commentary in the next chapter.

Why So Many Commentaries?

There certainly are a lot of commentaries around. There are so many, in fact, that it would be prohibitively time-consuming for anyone to consult all the hundreds of commentaries in existence on any given passage. This book deals only with English language commentaries, of which there are thousands. We've actually listed more than 1,100. When you add the non-English commentaries, from Japanese to Russian to German to Portuguese and scores of other languages, you have a huge group indeed—tens of thousands since the advent of the printing press.

Two words summarize the reason for the large variety of commentaries published around the world: people and purposes. People buy commentaries. It costs plenty of money and takes a lot of time to publish a commentary, and no publisher would think of undertaking a commentary project, small or large, unless it believed that there would be sufficient demand for the commentary to cover the cost of its publication. People generate that demand, because they want to understand what they are reading in the Bible. Who are these people? Well, they are any persons who have a strong desire to know more than they can figure out on their own just by reading the Bible. And that, of course, is their purpose.

At the top of the list are pastors of churches. They have the task of speaking at length every week on passages in the Bible, and most of them are well aware that without commentaries they would be at a disadvantage in speaking accurately about the Bible. Most American pastors own dozens of individual commentary volumes. Most also try to have at least one complete set of commentaries, i.e., a multi-volume series covering all the books of the Bible.

Church teachers are probably the second largest group using commentaries. They buy the single-volume commentaries more often than anything else. Again, their weekly demands for information about biblical texts lead them to an interest in commentaries. Bible study leaders (and informed participants) are a third group. Since nearly all Bible studies are passage oriented, commentaries are a useful aid to interpretation. Because Bible studies tend to avoid large books of the Bible and also tend to avoid those books that are trickier to interpret or harder to plow through, these people tend to buy mainly popular (e.g., paperback) commentaries on individual books of the Bible, and not complete sets or comprehensive one-volume commentaries.

Students are another group—theological students because they are learning to preach and teach and commentaries help them in their tasks, and college students because commentaries help them in their Bible courses. The latter group buy mostly what their professors tell them to!

There is also a large miscellaneous category of commentary users, composed of people who may not have formal responsibilities in teaching, preaching, leading Bible studies, or taking courses in biblical studies, but who want to learn rightly what the Bible says and are happy to have any help they can get in the process. What sorts of commentaries they will use is a matter of what their educational and interest levels are. The wise pastor, teacher, or Bible study leader should be aware, however, that these folks may come to church or Bible study knowing more about the passage to be preached on or studied than the one doing the preaching, teaching, or leading. That's when the priesthood of all believers puts some good, healthy pressure on the person who thinks he or she doesn't need to prepare the passage all that carefully.

Who Decides that Commentaries Should Be Produced?

The publishers do. Individual scholars may offer to write commentaries, but publishers decide what will actually appear in print, because they must foot the bill for the huge costs of editing, printing, paper, binding, advertising, stocking, and shipping. Thus another reason that there are so many commentaries is that there are many publishers of religious books willing to print them. Each one has built up a clientele, a "market" not exactly shared by any other publisher. This is a very healthy situation, since various publishers will invite various scholars to write commentaries for them. This tends to create a climate in which fresh research is sponsored and in which the natural competition for readership prods scholars to write books that people can profit from, not merely books that will make the scholars look good in the eyes of their peers. The system is not foolproof, of course, but at least it tends to prevent the unoriginal, monolithic commentaries that we might get if there were fewer publishers or no competition among them.

Moreover, publishers don't just have one market; they have several. Some publishers may attempt to reach only a very narrow, homogeneous group of people with their books, but most have a broader strategy. They want to reach the various kinds of people who have differing interests with regard to Bible learning. As an example, take Word Books, the publisher of the guidebook you are reading right now. Word publishes commentaries at a variety of levels, and for a variety of audiences.

I have had the privilege of writing two of my commentaries for Word, two very different kinds of commentaries, in two of the various series in which they have published commentaries. One was a commentary in a scholarly, technical series called the Word Biblical Commentary. It is based directly on the original languages, and includes extensive attention to original language textual analysis, literary analysis, historical background, semantics, grammar, theological implications, and other specialized issues. Commentaries in this series are of an in-depth type; there are in all fifty-two volumes, each several hundred pages in length, each having lengthy bibliographies and extensive references to scholarly literature. The editors of the series are scholars, seminary professors like myself. They approached me to write the first volume on the Minor Prophets (Hosea through Jonah), knowing me mainly as a fellow professor and scholar, and thinking of my technical abilities in that light. They provided scores of pages of detailed instructions for each contributor aimed at insuring that the series would provide the highest possible level of scholarship for the benefit of pastors, seminary students, and others. Each contributor is obliged to follow those instructions so that every volume in the series will reflect the concern of the editors that it be "the best of critical evangelical scholarship."

But that's only one kind of commentary. The other commentary I have written for Word Books was on Ezekiel, for a series called the Communicator's Commentary. That's a series of homiletical commentaries (commentaries written mainly to offer suggestions on how to illustrate the Bible in sermons) that is sufficiently specialized that it is not represented much in the listings that come later in this guidebook. It is a series edited not by a professor but by a gifted pastor, and all the volumes are written by preachers— with preachers especially in mind as an audience. I was asked to contribute to this series not because of my scholarly ability, but because of my experience as a preacher. (In addition to being a seminary professor I am the pastor of a church.) The fact that I was a seminary professor was pretty much irrelevant to the editor and publisher (though certainly not to me). The instructions to the commentators were different because the series had a different target audience. Here the concern was to help the reader to see the passage from an experienced preacher's viewpoint.

Both of these contrasting commentary series, as well as the other commentary series that Word Books publishes, have value, but for differing purposes. For example, in the volumes of the Word Biblical Commentary you won't get many direct suggestions for sermon or lesson illustrations on your passage. What you will get is a detailed, high-level analysis of the issues confronted in the various passages, which ought to help you preach or teach accurately. In the Communicator's Commentary, on the other hand, you won't get many answers to technical questions such as archaeological evidence or textual corruptions or the biblical author's intent. What you will get is a look at how people known for their communication skills thought the passages could be highlighted. With regard to my own commentaries in these two series, I have not set out to make one of them "better" than the other. They simply have different purposes. For answering questions about the passage, the Word Biblical Commentary is the series to consult. For a look at how a well-known evangelical preacher saw the potential for emphasizing the passage in a sermon, the Communicator's Commentary would be more appropriate. Publishers publish different commentaries for different people's differing needs.

Accuracy the Motivation

Above all else, it is the desire for accuracy that should be the driving force behind commentary use. After all, no matter how interesting or memorable or otherwise impressive a sermon or lesson or Bible study might be, if it isn't accurate it just isn't any good. If it's wrong, you've done everyone a disservice, no matter how "fascinating" or "exciting" people might find your words.

I'm not sure that the desire for accuracy actually is the motivation for commentary use in all instances, however. Quite often the real motive is the desire for "ideas"—or "suggestions" as people sometimes put it—that is, for stimulation toward an effective, captivating presentation of the material in the passage rather than for a correct and proper understanding of it. Under the pressure of needing "something more to say" about a passage, people will turn to commentaries to see what ideas they might get to fill out the time allotted for their sermon or lesson.

Regardless of the original motivation, however, we can always hope that the commentary consulter will end up being more accurate *and* interesting, never merely more interesting. And since the vast majority of commentaries are written for the purpose of helping clarify Scripture passages rather than for the purpose of making them somehow more exciting to an audience, when we talk about commentaries we are naturally talking about accuracy much more than about interest. It may be noted, by the way, that what many people mean by "interesting" when they evaluate a sermon or lesson is that the *non*-biblical material held their interest. They liked, in other words, the stories and other illustrative material that may have been presented rather than the biblical content itself. I'm hoping that no one reading this book has come to it with that sort of purpose in mind.

Some Standard Components of Commentaries

Virtually any English-language commentary you can buy will have certain characteristics that can be called "standard" in a commentary.

An Introduction

First, almost all commentaries have an introduction section, in which you are given a basic orientation to the biblical book (or portion thereof) that the commentary is written to explain. The commentator here summarizes what can be known or assumed about the human author(s) of the biblical book, the time or times in which it was written, its general content, its structure, its major unique features, and so on. These introductions, which usually constitute from 2 to 10 percent of a commentary's total length, are quite important reading because the introduction is the only place that most commentators talk systematically about the book they are commenting on *as a whole*. Knowing the fragments is one thing—very desirable. Knowing the whole as a whole is another—also very desirable.

Attention to Translation

Most commentaries follow the biblical text in order, section by section (passage by passage). Many offer their own translations of the biblical text, or at least occasional translation comments or suggestions. The most technical, and thus usually the most detailed commentaries, will also add explanations of the translation and even textual decisions made by the commentator. This is often provided in a section labeled "Notes to the Translation" or the like.

Selectivity

While nearly all detailed commentaries talk about individual verses, that's not because the commentator thinks that the verse divisions are reliable, but because the verse divisions are the only agreed-upon means available to identify small sections of text. Almost never, however, will a commentator discuss equally all the words or phrases in a verse. He or she will invariably concentrate on some and ignore others, because to do otherwise would be to insult the reader's intelligence. You don't want every noun, adjective, verb, adverb, article, etc., expounded for you. You don't want the commentator to say, "Here again, we have the word *the* in front of the word *road* because it was not just any road in the world that they were walking on but a specific road . . ." You want, instead, for the commentator to select those things that need clarification and comment carefully on them, rather than on everything, whether obvious or not.

The same kind of selectivity is necessary in the case of larger chunks of text—groups of verses or entire passages. Commentaries are *always* selective in what they choose to comment on. Keep that in mind. Often, the commentator's judgment will be much more important to you than his or her narrow technical ability. Most commentators know enough to write about much more than they do. You want to be sure that what the commentator has chosen to say is what you want to hear. What good does it do you to read a commentary that discusses brilliantly and in enormous detail things you don't need to find out?

More Attention to the More Difficult Parts

With regard to selectivity, nearly all commentaries devote more space to important or tricky verses than they do to those that are easy to understand or not likely to raise questions in the readers' minds (such as the long genealogies in Chronicles). However, here's a place where you need to be on guard, because poor commentaries often do just the opposite. One mark of a bad commentary is that it will belabor the obvious while glossing over the difficult or highly significant parts of the text.

Referral to Other Literature

Most commentaries also give you at least some idea of other things you can read about the book (and/or passage) that the commentary is written on. A commentary without a bibliography or notes referring to other sources of information, ancient or modern, including the work of other scholars, is not likely very thorough, and its views should be judged accordingly. This is not to say that the best commentaries are the ones with the longest bibliographies and most references—but some bibliography or references normally will be helpful to you.

Lack of Printed Illustrations

Most commentaries lack pictures, and few have even charts. This is neither good nor bad, but merely a typical characteristic. The Bible itself contains no pictures or charts, so commentaries, which are therefore about words rather than pictures, tend to follow suit.

Supplemental Information

Finally, it is characteristic of a commentary to supplement the biblical text. In one sense, supplementation is the heart and soul of a commentary. That's right—a commentary by its very nature adds information that the biblical text does not supply. This is absolutely necessary, yet terribly dangerous at the same time. Here's the problem: Since we live in a different age, place, and culture from any of the Bible writers or their original audiences, we cannot automatically understand everything they said. There are barriers of understanding (language, vocabulary, idiomatic expressions, historical and cultural background, experience, etc.) between us, and somehow these barriers have to be overcome. But it is not always obvious exactly what information will be relevant or appropriate to do the job. How do we answer the question: "What supplemental information do people need in order to understand a passage that is presently unclear to them?"

Consider this example: When the original audience of exiled Jews in Mesopotamia heard Ezekiel sing an allegorical lament about the past kings of Judah (Ezekiel 19), they knew when it began and when it ended and what it was about. His song was in the form of a funerary lament, and they had heard such funerary lament songs all their lives, and were also well used to prophetic symbolism. Moreover, they knew their own national history, including the major events in the lives of their recent kings. But the average modern person is almost completely unfamiliar with such things. When he or she reads Ezekiel 19, he or she *needs to know* some things that the chapter does not explicitly contain, but which Ezekiel and his audience knew well, or the chapter will remain a puzzle.

Allow me to use, again, one of my own commentaries as an illustration of how a commentary writer might try to address this concern. In my recent commentary on Ezekiel (in the Communicator's Commentary series mentioned above) I felt obliged to provide a lot of supplemental information about Ezekiel 19—information that the biblical text itself does *not* contain—for the very purpose of being sure that my readers would understand what the biblical text *does* contain. For example, I considered it my responsibility to describe for the reader how funerary laments are structured. The Bible never tells you that—it simply has a lot of such laments in it. But scholars have figured out by careful analysis what kinds of laments there are in the Bible and generally how they are structured, and the results of their work are easily available in books and articles.

Having read those books and articles and having done some further analysis of my own, I think I have a clear, accurate way of identifying the significant features of a funerary lament. So I've included a brief analysis of those features, as they are found in the lament song itself, in my comments on Ezekiel 19, an allegorical funerary lament. Naturally, I take the time to comment on how the passage is not literal but allegorical—again, something that the original audience knew at once, but which a modern reader might not realize.

In addition, I tell the readers of my commentary which kings (called "princes" by Ezekiel) are alluded to in the chapter. Ezekiel himself never identifies them. I do. Why? Because I think that you, the reader, need to have the kind of supplemental information that Ezekiel's ancient audience had when they heard the words from the prophet's mouth. They already knew a good many things—things that Ezekiel did not have to tell them—that made it possible for them to understand God's word as he preached it to them. You and I need to know those same things or we just won't understand what this portion of the word of God is getting at. So, to the extent that I believe I know which bits and pieces of supplemental information you will need to understand Ezekiel 19 accurately, I pass them along to you in my commentary. Then we can both understand God's word, which is my goal as a commentary writer and, I hope, your goal as a reader.

The Problem of Trusting the Commentator

But note this: You have to trust me to supply you the right supplemental information. There's no question that you need supplemental information to be on a comprehension level equal to that of the original audience, and thus to understand the passage. The only question is: Have I given you the right information? Maybe I have misanalyzed that chapter. Maybe I don't know as much about allegories as I think I do. Maybe I missed something about funerary laments in my past study that would, if I had only known it, have caused me to interpret the passage differently. Maybe I identified the wrong kings. Maybe I took the passage as alluding to one era in Judah's history when in fact a whole different era was intended. How do you know? Well, for that answer you ought to read the next chapter of this guidebook. But even before you do, you can help to safeguard yourself to a considerable degree against the possibility that a commentator has supplied you with misleading information, by following the "golden rule of commentary use."

Golden Rule of Commentary Use

It's simple: *Always consult more than one commentary on your passage.* Be sure to get a second opinion. Nobody is always right. No commentator is so free of bias and so full of knowledge that he or she will invariably be able to explain the meaning of biblical passages faultlessly. I can assure you that all of us who write commentaries change our minds about how passages are to be understood (and thus in the second edition revise things that we said in the first), are only barely sure of ourselves about other passages, and sometimes are completely puzzled about points in a passage, if not the passage itself. (It would be highly unlikely that a commentator would have no idea what to do with an entire passage. But there are plenty of whole verses that I don't think anyone has yet figured out—and I haven't hesitated to admit that in my commentaries when such verses were under discussion.) A good commentator will always be honest with you about the degree of certainty that applies to his or her comments. Beware of the cocksure commentator, who never lets on that there is anything unknown.

Getting a second opinion won't absolutely guarantee that you will never be led astray, but it's the best way to be as sure as you can. Compare and contrast what commentary B says about the passage with what commentary A says about it. Where do they agree? Where don't they? Does A talk about things that B ignores or vice versa? Is B more hesitant than A? Does one provide supplemental data that the other leaves out? Ask questions that force you to compare at least two commentaries on your passage. It works. Always get a second opinion.

2

The Types and Sizes of Commentaries, and How to Choose among Them

Although every commentary is somewhat unique, there is a quick way to describe virtually any commentary clearly enough that its basic characteristics will be understood. By using only four basic measurements or "yardsticks" we can categorize most commentaries reasonably well. The four yardsticks are:

Four Basic Yardsticks

1. Size
2. Detail
3. Level
4. Theology

If you have a general idea of (1) the size of a commentary, and you know (2) how detailed its comments are relative to the biblical text, and (3) what level of readership it is written to appeal to, as well as (4) the overall theological conviction of its author, you can reasonably say that you understand what sort of commentary it is.

Of course, the four yardsticks require some delineation, and this is easily accomplished. Each yardstick may be divided into three or four rankings, as follows:

1. Size
    a. One-to-all
    b. One-to-several
    c. One-to-one

2. *Detail*
    a. Summary
    b. Semi-detailed
    c. Detailed
    d. In-depth
3. *Level*
    a. Popular
    b. Serious
    c. Technical
4. *Theology*
    a. Evangelical
    b. Conservative-moderate
    c. Liberal

Let's explain what we mean when we talk about these rankings within the four basic yardsticks:

The Size Yardstick

When we talk about "one-to-all," "one-to-several," and "one-to-one," here's what we mean:

A *one-to-all* commentary is almost always a collection of short commentaries written by a single author (rarely) or variety of authors (typically) on various books and combined in a *single* large volume. An example of this type of commentary is *The New Bible Commentary, Revised* (InterVarsity). This type of commentary, also known as a single-volume commentary, covers an entire Testament or the entire Bible. When you purchase a commentary of this kind, you get everything in one volume, and the comments on any given book can't possibly be very lengthy. Also, you must take the good with the bad—excellent commentaries on some books are likely to be bound together with undesirable commentaries on other books.

A *one-to-several* commentary is a commentary on several books of the Bible. Typically, one author will cover one, two, or more biblical books in his or her portion of the whole commentary, and a general editor will organize the various authors' commentaries together into a group. A single volume may thus contain several individual commentaries by several different authors. An example of this type of commentary set is the Expositor's Bible Commentary (Zondervan). Commentaries of this sort are often called "multi-volume sets" or the like, and the word "commentary" can apply to the whole set as well as to any of the individual commentaries within the set. A complete one-to-several commentary set covers a Testament or the entire Bible. Greater length is possible for each biblical book's commentary than is the case with the one-to-all commentaries, and only a few book commentaries are bound together in each of the volumes. This kind of set allows you, then, to purchase just the volume on, say, the Gospels, or the Pentateuch, rather than buying volumes on parts of the Bible you may not want to study at the moment.

A *one-to-one* commentary is a commentary that itself is a single book, written on a single Bible book (or portion of a Bible book, or group of short books). Such commentaries are most often found in series, which may have as many as forty or fifty volumes altogether. Sometimes, this sort of commentary will actually include in a single volume more than one biblical book, mainly in the case of groups of shorter biblical books that, taken together, are roughly equal to a more average-sized biblical book. In commentaries of this sort, for example, it is almost routine to find a single volume devoted to several of the Minor Prophets, or to Ezra and Nehemiah together, or to all three of the letters of John, or to 2 Peter and Jude together. In that case, we still refer to the commentaries as "one-to-one" commentaries, since the *typical* volume in such a set covers only a single average-length biblical book. On the other hand, a long book like Psalms or Isaiah may be covered in two or more volumes. Instances of this type of commentary would be the Tyndale Old Testament Commentary or the Tyndale New Testament Commentary (most of whose volumes are either detailed or semi-detailed, serious, and evangelical; published by Eerdmans and InterVarsity) and the Word Biblical Commentary (in-depth, technical, and mostly evangelical, published by Word).

Rarely, one even encounters a complete commentary volume on a single important portion of a biblical book, such as the Sermon on the Mount. An example of this would be R. Guelich's *The Sermon on the Mount* (Word Books), which is a huge commentary just on chapters 5, 6, and 7 of Matthew. The ratio of comment to passage is enormous in a commentary like Guelich's, but for convenience we include it in our "one-to-one" category, since aside from its great concentration on such a relatively small part of one biblical book, the reader would not find it substantially different in characteristics from the sorts of commentaries people think of when they have in mind what we are calling one-to-one commentaries. Sometimes, such a commentary is independent of a set, i.e., just a single-volume commentary on a single biblical book—or perhaps even a portion of a single book.

The Detail Yardstick

Our four ranks within this yardstick are "summary," "semi-detailed," "detailed," and "in-depth." Here is what we mean by them:

A *summary* commentary is relatively short compared to the biblical book it is written to explain. Generally the commentary will contain a summation of the passage and any specific observations that the commentator might feel are important to make, but not much else. Usually such commentaries contain fewer words of comment on the biblical text in question than are found in the biblical text itself. The commentator, in other words, has room only to summarize his or her points in this kind of commentary. Most of the one-volume commentaries are of this type. Their comments are typically restricted to large blocks of text, since they simply don't have the space to comment routinely on individual verses or even on small groups of verses. They can perhaps discuss a very few especially significant individual verses by themselves, but never at great length. These commentaries are intended to provide the reader with an overview of the biblical text, not with detailed discussion of its content at each point.

A *semi-detailed* commentary is one in which the space allowed for the author's comments is definitely limited, but in which the author at least has enough room to make comments about small blocks of text, and frequently a sentence or two about individual verses. Many, though not all, of the several-volume commentaries (one-to-several) are of this type. Semi-detailed commentaries normally concentrate on small blocks of text, a few verses at a time, and may include brief discussions of most individual verses. The Cambridge Bible Commentary on the New English Bible is an example of a semi-detailed commentary series.

Detailed commentaries almost always say something about each verse, although they may do so within discussions of small blocks of text. Some verses may be covered in great detail, and the introductions and indexes of such commentaries are usually fairly detailed as well. The volumes in the series called Harper's New Testament Commentaries fall mostly into the "detailed" commentary category.

In an *in-depth* commentary, passages are still the dominant factor, but the author has been allowed the freedom to analyze individual verses at length, so that virtually any medium-sized or long verse will receive detailed comment. In fact, the only verses not receiving individual attention on a verse-by-verse basis will be those that are so short, repetitive, or routine that two or more are lumped together for discussion. But that is the exception, not the rule. For the most part, every verse is treated to some degree separately, and especially significant verses may be analyzed for several pages if necessary. The writers of in-depth commentaries are either not held to page limits, or are given limits so generous that they can say virtually all that they feel must be said about any word, sentence, verse, or passage. An in-depth commentary tries, then, to say everything relevant about all the verses of a biblical book, may contain extensive introductory sections and indexes, and is written with the intent to provide full, thorough coverage of any issues that might pertain to the biblical book being commented on. The Hermeneia series and the Word Biblical Commentary series are examples of in-depth commentaries.

The Level Yardstick

With regard to the *level* that a commentary may be written at, the three rankings we believe differentiate best among types are "popular," "serious," and "technical."

Popular commentaries assume virtually no knowledge of the biblical material, and try to explain for the reader what the text says in the simplest of terms. Most of the time these commentaries consciously avoid discussing topics and facts that are so complicated as to require further reading to appreciate fully. In other words, popular commentaries provide conscious simplifications of the material, and omit much that might be discussed, so as to be readable by almost any adult who reads books. Since fewer than 10 percent of literate adult Americans regularly read books (their reading being limited mainly to magazines and newspapers) these commentaries are not appealing to just anyone, but to people whose interest level is already beyond a casual level. They are "popular" in design, even though hardly universally used.

A popular commentary is non-technical. It requires almost no Bible knowledge to use, and is written specifically for what is usually called a "general" audience—people who may well be starting out in their study of the Bible, or at least of the book the commentary is written on. The Bible Study Commentary series is an example of a set of "popular" commentaries.

Serious commentaries are written for those who want to study a biblical text with some degree of care and desire to understand it more than on a surface level, but who may not be able to or may not choose to concern themselves with technical issues like the wording of the original languages, the complications of textual matters, and extensive reference to scholarly literature. In such commentaries, you will not normally find any of the Hebrew, Aramaic, or Greek text printed, though you might find individual words referred to in transliteration (written out in English alphabetical letters). A serious commentary is partly technical and presumes some Bible knowledge on the part of the reader, but it does not require the reader to know the original language of the biblical book being commented on. A serious commentary usually refers at least sporadically to other parts of the Bible, to relevant history, to comparative literature, and to secondary literature (other commentaries, books, and articles on the same biblical book). The Tyndale Old Testament and New Testament Commentaries fit the "serious" category.

Technical commentaries are just that—highly technical. They tend to refer routinely to the original languages, on which they are based. The author thus comments throughout the commentary about the Hebrew, Aramaic, or Greek text—not about the English translation, except where he or she feels the need to correct a common English mistranslation, for example. To appreciate these commentaries in the fullest manner, you need to know the original, and read them with your original language text open. Such commentaries also address in detail the issues of textual accuracy, forms, structure, and cultural setting, and also tend to interact substantially with the opinions of other scholars. Thus you may expect to find in a technical commentary frequent reference to scholarly books and journal articles, as well as ample bibliographies.

Such a commentary is consciously aimed at the person who knows the original language of the biblical book being written on, who wants to read about what other scholars have discovered about the book, and who is interested in and capable of appreciating such technical matters as original-language grammar and translation issues, textual issues (the determination of the exact original wording by the comparison of all existing manuscripts) and so forth. Technical commentaries require seminary or advanced college-level biblical training to appreciate fully. This does not mean, however, that parts of them aren't quite useful to a non-professional reader willing to work at understanding the biblical text. Virtually any volume in the International Critical Commentary, Hermeneia, the Word Biblical Commentary, or the New International Greek Testament Commentary will serve as an example of a technical commentary.

The Yardstick of Theology

Our fourth yardstick, *theology*, has three ranks: evangelical, conservative-moderate, and liberal. Because theology is usually a matter of strongly held opinions, this category is bound to be the most controversial. But it cannot be ignored. There is no such thing as being "neutral" about the Bible, and people interested in commentaries are almost never indifferent to commentators' theological stances. Here is what we mean when we use these three terms:

Evangelical commentaries are written by authors who regard the Bible as fully inspired by God, the very word of God given through human beings. Such commentators therefore will not, except by reason of ignorance or accident, treat anything that the Bible states as incorrect. Of course, all sorts of people who are quoted in the Bible may make incorrect statements but that is very different from saying that anything the Bible itself states as fact is incorrect. Evangelical commentators are bound to take extremely seriously anything that the Bible teaches, and will openly and consciously defend its accuracy against presumptions to the contrary. The New International Commentary on the Old Testament and the New International Commentary on the New Testament are, in most of their volumes, evangelical.

Conservative-moderate commentaries are authored by persons who may regard the Bible as generally or usually factual and in some way (not always well defined) inspired, but who believe that it has at many places faults and errors, the product of human limitation. These commentaries downplay the divine side of the inspiration process and play up the human side, tending to assume that the human side has been dominant in the production of the Bible. For example, a conservative-moderate commentator may talk routinely about Paul's insights *about* God, but will not tend to concern himself or herself very much about God's revelation *through* Paul. Interestingly, no series of which I am aware is consistently conservative-moderate. For individual examples, see the listings in chapter 3.

Liberal commentaries openly treat the Bible as a fully (or nearly so) human product, routinely discounting the reliability of its historical material and emphasizing what the commentary authors perceive as inconsistencies and contradictions within the text. Liberal commentators tend to perceive differing theologies both within and among the biblical books, and they tend to highlight this. Their interest is usually in variety rather than unity, and as a result the commentaries they write do not normally have any interest in answering a question like, "How can we obey/respond to what the Bible says here?"

Liberal commentators are often brilliantly insightful, because the Bible is not a mystery book. While it is necessary to believe the Bible to appreciate all of it, it is not necessary to believe it to understand many parts of it. A mystery book would be a book unclear to all but those who have the special key to understand it. This is not at all the case with the Bible, which nowhere says that it cannot be understood by nonbelievers or those highly skeptical of parts of it. The Bible points out that many important elements of the Christian faith are foolishness to the nonbeliever, but this is very different from saying that what the Bible says is somehow not clear to nonbelievers. They can understand it clearly and still regard belief in it as foolish.

Liberals, therefore, in spite of their tendency to dismiss many parts of the Bible as factually unreliable, have often discovered things about the Bible as the result of diligent study that the rest of us who *do* have a higher view of its accuracy are delighted to add to our knowledge. This guidebook, accordingly, will include liberal commentaries among its listings, in light of their great usefulness to those who have a higher view of the reliability of the Bible. The volumes in the International Critical Commentary, the Old Testament Message, the New Testament Message, the Old Testament Library, the Interpreter's Bible, and Hermeneia are nearly all examples of theologically liberal commentaries.

Are There Other Categories?

Sometimes additional criteria characterize a commentary, further distinguishing it beyond the characterizations provided via the four yardsticks mentioned above. Nearly always, these additional criteria will apply when the publishers and writers of a single commentary volume or a commentary series have consciously set out to produce a commentary with a special slant. Their desire may have been to create something atypical—specialized in some way for a unique audience. For example, there are "theological commentaries," which largely downplay questions other than the theological connections of the passages in a biblical book to the greater "theological encyclopedia," i.e., the systematic coverage of all theological beliefs held by Christians in general or some denomination or branch thereof. Some series that their publishers call "theological commentaries," however, are nothing more than fairly typical commentaries with an interest in theology—something any good commentary should have automatically.

There are also "homiletical commentaries," in which the main interest is in providing preachers with ways to illustrate the biblical material in sermons and lessons. Sadly, the underlying but never openly expressed assumption of most such commentaries is that the Bible itself doesn't do a very good job of communicating its own message. As a result, most exegetes (those interested in close, careful analysis of the meaning of biblical passages) and homileticians (experts in preaching) usually don't recommend homiletical commentaries. I won't be recommending any series of this type in this guidebook, either, because none I have ever come across is sufficiently accurate in clarifying the biblical text to be commended to the reader.

Some commentaries have a special theological slant that sets them apart (and may sometimes limit their audience). An example would be the Wesleyan Bible Commentary, a one-to-several, semi-detailed, serious, evangelical commentary that defends the particular doctrines of the Wesleyan theological tradition (the freedom of the human will to reject the will of God, a strong emphasis on holy living rather than capitulation to sin as inevitable, etc.). Such commentaries are not automatically either good or bad, unless their authors attempt to manipulate the biblical data to fit their own preconceptions—and that can happen with any commentary.

Archaeological or linguistic commentaries are likewise specialized to the point of having a slant that sets them apart from typical commentaries. Archaeological commentaries concentrate on the evidence from archaeological research that may illuminate a passage. Naturally, passages in the historical books that mention places, objects, and cultural practices get more attention in such commentaries than do those parts of the Bible whose subject matter is more strictly "theological." Linguistic commentaries are concerned with those issues that will affect proper translation, and little else. They have great value to the translator, but limited value for the Bible student whose purposes are more general.

The Theory of Choosing the Right Commentary

Once you know the categories that commentaries fall into, and you can describe a commentary by its "yardsticks," you are in a very strong position to choose a commentary, or commentaries, according to (1) how much you already know and (2) what you're trying to learn.

The point here is that different people need different commentaries for different purposes. Suppose you want to study the Greek text of 1 Peter and can devote an hour a day for a month to doing so. A "popular" level commentary will not serve your purposes. You'd be largely wasting your time with such a commentary—not because it isn't excellent in its own right, but because it just isn't aimed at the purpose you have in mind. What you want is a commentary that has a lot of detail, that focuses on the original language, and that gives a comprehensive analysis of the exegetical issues in 1 Peter.

On the other hand, suppose you are preparing a single, one-hour topical Bible study on "The Godly Wife and Mother." You may need to consult a commentary or commentaries on a dozen or more passages that you have selected to comprise the focus of the Bible study, and even a major passage like Proverbs 31:10–31 will be merely one of the many passages you will be obliged to include. If you want an easy-to-digest overview of Proverbs 31 but have only ten or fifteen minutes to read through a commentary on it, an in-depth technical commentary will almost certainly be too long and too detailed for you to meet your deadline, unless you are already a well-trained Bible student (e.g., a pastor who graduated from a seminary like the one I teach at) who can skim through the many pages devoted to that passage, reading *selectively* the parts that answer your questions or fill in gaps in your already substantial knowledge about Proverbs.

This doesn't mean that whenever you are pressed for time you ought to go right to the lowest common denominator in commentaries, i.e., a one-to-all, summary, popular commentary. But it does mean that such a commentary may be exactly what you will often want to start with, in order to obtain a quick overview of the significant data that bear upon the passage(s) you are seeking information about.

Don't rely solely or substantially upon a commentary written by one person on the whole Bible or a whole Testament. The advantage of such commentaries is that they are consistent, and often written by someone gifted at making things clear. The disadvantage, however, is that they can hardly contain as much accurate information as a commentary written by several commentators, for two reasons. First, it is simply not possible for one person to master enough information to be good at analyzing the whole Bible or a whole Testament. Second, it is likely that to avoid repetition, the single author of a full commentary will fail to mention in one place (e.g. the letters of Paul) something he or she has already discussed at length earlier—say in the Gospels. So unless you read from cover to cover through these, you miss a lot that has already been said, or that is being saved by the author for inclusion at some later point.

Actually Choosing a Commentary: Seven Things You Can Do

Finally, here are seven things you can, and indeed ought to, do when you look at a commentary to consider whether or not you want to buy it, borrow it, or check it out from the library:

1. *Check the table of contents* to see how comprehensive its topics are.

2. *Check the index* to see the range of subjects it treats.

3. *Check the bibliographies* it provides. Are these helpful to the extent that you want out of such a commentary?

4. *Flip through the commentary to see its overall detail and level.* You can tell at a glance if the author is referring to the original languages much or at all, and can see in a few seconds of reading if the author refers to extrabiblical passages and languages frequently, occasionally, or not at all. You can tell fairly easily if this is a commentary in which the author interacts with other parts of the Bible, if he or she gives you useful bibliographical references (i.e., to what extent he or she is in dialogue with the current secondary literature), and so forth.

5. *Read a sample portion* to see if it's clear and comprehensive, and to see how many facts and how much data the author has given

about the passage. It is an especially good idea to check out the way the author treats a passage you know something about.

6. *Pick a controversial verse or small unit* from a passage—a verse or unit that you know isn't easy to interpret, and skim through what the author says about it. If you are still left with questions, or if the author doesn't treat it at all, you know what kind of depth of discussion the commentary is likely to contain. A good commentary for your purposes is always one that covers the things you are wondering about.

7. *Try to assess the theological slant* of the author by skimming over what he or she says about some part of the book that you know is not assumed to be true or accurate by everyone. Those places where a biblical book speaks of the supernatural (predictive prophecies, miracle stories, statements of faith in life after death, etc.) are good test points to read. It is not necessary to reject a commentary just because it doesn't fit your theology, but it may be a good idea to balance a non-evangelical commentary with an evangelical one if you are, in fact, looking for help in building up your faith in the God of the Scriptures.

3

Selected Commentary List
Arranged by Book of the Bible

In the last one hundred years many thousands of commentaries have been published in the English language. Just over 1,100 of them are listed here. There is good reason for this selectivity.

I have not listed commentaries that I thought were (1) not likely to stay in print or were so long out of print that they would not be generally accessible to readers; (2) not widely available for any other reason; (3) not reliable; (4) not sufficiently high in quality or consistent in quality to warrant listing; (5) published so close to the time of the writing of this book that I didn't have time to include them; or (6) specialized commentaries, according to the definition of specialized commentaries given in the Preface. There are, undoubtedly, some commentaries that I have accidentally not listed. I'll try to correct accidental oversights in future editions of this book.

Please note: The fact that I list a commentary here does not mean that I think that its views are correct or that I think it could or should be in everyone's library. Many of the commentaries listed are ones whose conclusions I would take strong exception to. My questions as I considered including a commentary in this list were simply: (1) Is it actually a commentary according to the definition stated earlier in this book? (2) Is it written by someone genuinely qualified to write on this part of the Bible? (3) Is it factual enough to contain a reasonable amount of information useful to all readers regardless of its theological stance? (4) Does it genuinely try to explain the text, even if from a perspective disagreeable to me personally? (5) Is it not so rare that almost no one could find a copy? In other words, is there a reasonable chance that medium-sized libraries would have, or be able to obtain for their borrowers, a copy? (6) Would it help an interested reader understand the Bible better and refer that reader appropriately to other useful books on the Bible? (7) Is it thorough enough and recent enough that its views are not out of date and not inadequately stated to the reader? If I could answer yes to these questions, I felt free to include a commentary in this list.

Note: The descriptions that follow the publication date in each listing are explained fully in chapter 2. The series abbreviations are explained in Appendix 2.

OLD TESTAMENT

Genesis

Baldwin, Joyce. *The Message of Genesis 12–50*. TBST. Leicester, England; Downers Grove, IL: InterVarsity, 1988. One-to-one, detailed, serious, evangelical.

Brueggemann, Walter. *Genesis*. INT. Louisville: Westminster/John Knox, 1982. One-to-one, detailed, serious, liberal.

Cassuto, Umberto. *From Adam to Noah: A Commentary on the Book of Genesis I–VI*. 3d ed. Trans. by I. Abrahams. New York: Magnes Press, 1978. One-to-one, in-depth, technical, conservative-moderate.

———. *From Noah to Abraham: A Commentary on the Book of Genesis VI–XI*. 3d ed. Trans. by I. Abrahams. New York: Magnes Press, 1984. One-to-one, in-depth, technical, conservative-moderate.

Keil, C. F., and Delitzsch, F. *The First Book of Moses (Genesis)*. K-D. Repr. Grand Rapids: Eerdmans, 1988. One-to-one, in-depth, technical, evangelical.

Kidner, Derek. *Genesis*. TOTC. Downers Grove, IL: InterVarsity, 1967. One-to-one, detailed, serious, evangelical.

Leupold, Herbert C. *Exposition of Genesis, Vol 1*. [Gen 1–19] Grand Rapids: Baker, 1956. One-to-one, semi-detailed, serious, evangelical.

———. *Exposition of Genesis, Vol 2*. [Gen 20–50] Grand Rapids: Baker, 1958. One-to-one, semi-detailed, serious, evangelical.

Maher, Michael, MSC. *Genesis*. OTM. Wilmington, DE: Michael Glazier, 1982. One-to-one, semi-detailed, serious, liberal.

McCurley, Foster. *Genesis, Exodus, Leviticus, Numbers*. PC. Philadelphia: Fortress, 1979. One-to-several, summary, serious, liberal.

Rad, Gerhard von. *Genesis, A Commentary.* 3d ed. OTL. Louisville: Westminster/John Knox, 1972. One-to-one, in-depth, technical, liberal.

Sailhamer, John. *Genesis.* EBC. Grand Rapids: Zondervan, 1989. One-to-several, detailed, serious, evangelical.

Sarna, Nahum. *Understanding Genesis.* New York: Schocken, 1966. One-to-one, semi-detailed, serious, liberal.

Simpson, Cuthbert. *Genesis.* IB. Nashville: Abingdon, 1952. One-to several, semi-detailed, technical, liberal.

Skinner, John. *Genesis.* ICC. Edinburgh: T. & T. Clark, 1910. One-to-one, in-depth, technical, liberal.

Speiser, E. A. *Genesis.* AB. Garden City: Doubleday, 1964. One-to-one, detailed, technical, liberal.

Wenham, Gordon. *Genesis 1–15.* WBC. Dallas, TX: Word Books, 1988. One-to-one, in-depth, technical, evangelical.

Westermann, Claus. *Genesis.* TAI. Grand Rapids: Eerdmans, 1987. One-to-one, detailed, serious, liberal.

———. *Genesis 1–11.* CC. Minneapolis: Augsburg, 1984. One-to-one, in-depth, technical, liberal.

———. *Genesis 12–36.* CC. Minneapolis: Augsburg, 1985. One-to-one, in-depth, technical, liberal.

———. *Genesis 37–50.* CC. Minneapolis: Augsburg, 1986. One-to-one, in-depth, technical, liberal.

Willis, John T. *Genesis.* Austin: Sweet, 1979. One-to-one, detailed, serious, evangelical.

Wood, Leon. *Genesis.* BSC. Grand Rapids: Zondervan, 1975. One-to-one, semi-detailed, popular, evangelical.

Exodus

Burns, Rita. *Exodus, Leviticus, Numbers with an Excursus on Feasts, Ritual, Typology.* OTM. Wilmington, DE: Michael Glazier, 1983. One-to-several, summary, serious, liberal.

Cassuto, Umberto. *A Commentary on the Book of Exodus.* 3d ed. New York: Magnes Press, 1983. One-to-one, in-depth, technical, conservative-moderate.

Childs, Brevard. *The Book of Exodus: A Critical, Theological Commentary.* OTL. Louisville: Westminster/John Knox, 1962. One-to-one, in-depth, technical, liberal.

Clements, Ronald E. *Exodus.* Cambridge: Cambridge University Press, 1972. One-to-one, detailed, technical, liberal.

Cole, R. Alan. *Exodus*. TOTC. Downers Grove, IL: InterVarsity, 1973. One-to-one, detailed, serious, evangelical.

Davies, G. Henton. *Exodus: Introduction and Commentary*. London: SCM Press, 1967. One-to-one, detailed, technical, liberal.

Durham, John I. *Exodus*. WBC. Waco, TX: Word Books, 1987. One-to-one, in-depth, technical, liberal.

Huey, F. B., Jr. *Exodus*. BSC. Grand Rapids: Zondervan, 1977. One-to-one, semi-detailed, popular, evangelical.

Hyatt, J. Philip. *Exodus*. NCBC. Grand Rapids: Eerdmans, 1980. One-to-one, in-depth, technical, liberal.

Kaiser, Walter, Jr. *Exodus*. EBC. Grand Rapids: Zondervan, 1989. One-to-several, detailed, serious, evangelical.

Keil, C. F., and Delitzsch, F. *The Second Book of Moses (Exodus)*. K-D. Repr. Grand Rapids: Eerdmans, 1988. One-to-one, in-depth, technical, evangelical.

McCurley, Foster: see Genesis.

Noth, Martin. *Exodus*. OTL. Philadelphia: Westminster, 1962. One-to-one, semi-detailed, technical, liberal.

Rylaarsdam, J. Coert. *Exodus*. IB. Nashville: Abingdon, 1952. One-to-several, semi-detailed, technical, liberal.

Leviticus

Burns, Rita: see Exodus.

Goldberg, Louis. *Leviticus*. BSC. Grand Rapids: Zondervan, 1980. One-to-one, semi-detailed, popular, evangelical.

Harris, R. Laird. *Leviticus*. EBC. Grand Rapids: Zondervan, 1989. One-to-several, detailed, serious, evangelical.

Harrison, R. K. *Leviticus*. TOTC. Downers Grove, IL: InterVarsity, 1980. One-to-one, detailed, serious, evangelical.

Keil, C. F., and Delitzsch, F. *The Third Book of Moses (Leviticus)*. K-D. Repr. Grand Rapids: Eerdmans, 1988. One-to-one, in-depth, technical, evangelical.

Mays, James L. *Leviticus*. LBC. Atlanta: John Knox, 1963. One-to-one, semi-detailed, serious, liberal.

McCurley, Foster: see Genesis.

Micklem, Nathaniel. *Leviticus*. IB. Nashville: Abingdon, 1952. One-to-several, semi-detailed, technical, liberal.

Noth, Martin. *Leviticus*. OTL. Philadelphia: Westminster, 1965. One-to-one, detailed, technical, liberal.

Porter, J. R. *Leviticus*. CBC. Cambridge: Cambridge University Press, 1976. One-to-one, detailed, serious, liberal.

Snaith, Norman H. *Leviticus and Numbers*. NCB. One-to-one, detailed, technical, liberal.

Wenham, Gordon J. *The Book of Leviticus*. NICOT. Grand Rapids: Eerdmans, 1979. One-to one, in-depth, technical, evangelical.

Numbers

Allen, Ronald. *Numbers*. EBC. Grand Rapids: Zondervan, 1990. One-to-several, detailed, serious, evangelical.

Budd, Philip J. *Numbers*. WBC. Waco, TX: Word Books, 1984. One-to-one, in-depth, technical, liberal.

Burns, Rita: see Exodus.

Gray, George Buchanan. *A Critical and Exegetical Commentary on Numbers*. ICC. Edinburgh: T. & T. Clark, 1903. One-to-one, in-depth, technical, liberal.

Huey, F. B., Jr. *Numbers*. BSC. Grand Rapids: Zondervan, 1981. One-to-one, semi-detailed, popular, evangelical.

Keil, C. F., and Delitzsch, F. *The Fourth Book of Moses (Numbers)*. K-D. Repr. Grand Rapids: Eerdmans, 1988. One-to-one, in-depth, technical, evangelical.

Maarsingh, B. *Numbers: A Practical Commentary*. TAI. Grand Rapids: Eerdmans, 1987. One-to-one, summary, serious, liberal.

Marsh, John. *Numbers*. IB. Nashville: Abingdon, 1952. One-to-several, semi-detailed, technical, liberal.

McCurley, Foster: see Genesis.

Noth, Martin. *Numbers*. OTL. Philadelphia: Westminster Press, 1968. One-to-one, detailed, technical, liberal.

Snaith, Norman H.: see Leviticus.

Sturdy, J. *Numbers*. CBCNEB. Cambridge: Cambridge University Press, 1972. One-to-one, semi-detailed, serious, liberal.

Wenham, Gordon. *Numbers*. TOTC. Downers Grove, IL: Inter-Varsity, 1982. One-to-one, detailed, serious, evangelical.

Deuteronomy

Achtemeier, Elizabeth. *Deuteronomy, Jeremiah*. PC. Philadelphia: Fortress Press, 1978. One-to-one, summary, serious, liberal.

Clifford, Richard, SJ. *Deuteronomy, with Excursus on Covenant and Law*. OTM. Wilmington, DE: Michael Glazier, 1982. One-to-one, semi-detailed, serious, liberal.

Craigie, Peter C. *The Book of Deuteronomy*. NICOT. Grand Rapids: Eerdmans, 1976. One-to one, in-depth, technical, evangelical.

Cunliffe-Jones, H. *Deuteronomy.* TBC. London: SCM, 1964. One-to-one, semi-detailed, technical, liberal.

Driver, S. R. *Deuteronomy.* 3d ed. ICC. Edinburgh: T. & T. Clark, 1901. One-to-one, in-depth, technical, liberal.

Goldberg, Louis. *Deuteronomy.* BSC. Grand Rapids: Zondervan, 1986. One-to-one, semi-detailed, popular, evangelical.

Keil, C. F., and Delitzsch, F. *The Fifth Book of Moses (Deuteronomy).* K-D. Repr. Grand Rapids: Eerdmans, 1988. One-to-one, in-depth, technical, evangelical.

Mayes, A. D. H. *Deuteronomy.* NCBC. Grand Rapids: Eerdmans, 1979. One-to-one, in-depth, technical, liberal.

Rad, Gerhard von. *Deuteronomy: A Commentary.* OTL. Louisville: Westminster/John Knox, 1966. One-to-one, detailed, technical, liberal.

Thompson, J. A. *Deuteronomy.* TOTC. Downers Grove, IL: Inter-Varsity, 1974. One-to-one, detailed, serious, evangelical.

Wright, G. Ernest. *Deuteronomy.* IB. Nashville: Abingdon, 1952. One-to-several, semi-detailed, technical, liberal.

Joshua

✓ Bright, John. *Joshua.* IB. Nashville: Abingdon, 1952. One-to-several, semi-detailed, technical, liberal.

✓ Butler, Trent. *Joshua.* WBC. Waco, TX: Word Books, 1983. One-to-one, in-depth, technical, conservative-moderate.

Enns, Paul. *Joshua.* BSC. Grand Rapids: Zondervan, 1982. One-to-one, semi-detailed, popular, evangelical.

Gray, John. *Joshua, Judges, Ruth.* Rev. ed. NCBC. Grand Rapids: Eerdmans, 1986. One-to-one, semi-detailed, technical, liberal.

Hoppe, Leslie, OFM. *Joshua, Judges, with Excursus on Charismatic Leadership in Israel.* OTM. Wilmington, DE: Michael Glazier, 1985. One-to-several, summary, serious, liberal.

Keil, C. F., and Delitzsch, F. *The Book of Joshua.* K-D. Repr. Grand Rapids: Eerdmans, 1988. One-to-one, in-depth, technical, evangelical.

Miller, J. M., and Tucker, Gene M. *Joshua.* CBCNEB. Cambridge: Cambridge University Press, 1974. One-to-one, semi-detailed, serious, liberal.

✓ Woudstra, Marten H. *The Book of Joshua.* NICOT. Grand Rapids: Eerdmans, 1981. One-to one, in-depth, technical, evangelical.

Judges

Boling, Robert G. *Judges.* AB. Garden City: Doubleday, 1975. One-to-one, detailed, technical, liberal.

Cundall, Arthur E., and Morris, Leon. *Judges and Ruth.* TOTC. Grand Rapids: Eerdmans, 1968. One-to-one, detailed, serious, evangelical.

Enns, Paul. *Judges.* BSC. Grand Rapids: Zondervan, 1982. One-to-one, semi-detailed, popular, evangelical.

Gray, John: see Joshua.

Hoppe, Leslie: see Joshua.

Keil, C. F., and Delitzsch, F. *The Book of Judges.* K-D. Repr. Grand Rapids: Eerdmans, 1988. One-to-one, in-depth, technical, evangelical.

Martin, J. D. *Judges.* CBCNEB. Cambridge: Cambridge University Press, 1975. One-to-one, semi-detailed, serious, liberal.

Moore, George F. *Judges.* 2d ed. ICC. Edinburgh: T. & T. Clark, 1895. One-to-one, in-depth, technical, liberal.

Myers, Jacob. *Judges.* IB. Nashville: Abingdon, 1952. One-to-several, semi-detailed, technical, liberal.

Soggin, J. Alberto. *Judges: A Commentary.* OTL. Louisville: Westminster/John Knox, 1981. One-to-one, in-depth, technical, liberal.

Ruth

Atkinson, David. *The Message of Ruth.* TBST. Downers Grove, IL: InterVarsity, 1983. One-to-one, semi-detailed, serious, evangelical.

Campbell, Edward F. *Ruth.* AB. Garden City: Doubleday, 1975. One-to-one, in-depth, technical, liberal.

Craghan, John: see Esther.

Cundall, Arthur, and Morris, Leon: see Judges.

Enns, Paul. *Ruth.* BSC. Grand Rapids: Zondervan, 1982. One-to-one, semi-detailed, popular, evangelical.

Fuerst, W. J. *Ruth, Esther, Ecclesiastes, Song of Songs, Lamentations.* CBCNEB. Cambridge: Cambridge University Press, 1975. One-to-several, semi-detailed, serious, liberal.

Gray, John: see Joshua.

Hubbard, Robert L., Jr. *The Book of Ruth.* NICOT. Grand Rapids: Eerdmans, 1990. One-to-one, in-depth, technical, evangelical.

Keil, C. F., and Delitzsch, F. *The Book of Ruth*. K-D. Repr. Grand Rapids: Eerdmans, 1988. One-to-one, in-depth, technical, evangelical.

Knight, George A. F. *Ruth and Jonah*. 2d ed. TBC. London: SCM Press, 1956. One-to-one, semi-detailed, serious, liberal.

Smith, Louise. *Ruth*. IB. Nashville: Abingdon, 1952. One-to-several, semi-detailed, technical, liberal.

1 Samuel

Ackroyd, Peter. *The First Book of Samuel*. CBCNEB. Cambridge and New York: Cambridge University Press, 1971. One-to-one, detailed, serious, liberal.

Baldwin, Joyce G. *1 and 2 Samuel*. TOTC. Downers Grove, IL: InterVarsity, 1988. One-to-one, semi-detailed, serious, evangelical.

Caird, George B. *The First and Second Books of Samuel*. IB. Nashville: Abingdon, 1953. One-to-several, semi-detailed, technical, liberal.

Conroy, Charles, MSC. *1–2 Samuel, 1–2 Kings, with Excursus on Davidic Dynasty and Holy City Zion*. OTM. Wilmington, DE: Michael Glazier, 1983. One-to-several, summary, serious, liberal.

Gehrke, R. D. *1 and 2 Samuel*. Concordia Commentary. St. Louis: Concordia, 1968. One-to-one, detailed, serious, conservative-moderate.

Goldman, S. *Samuel*. Soncino Books of the Bible. London: Soncino Press, 1951. One-to-one, detailed, technical, liberal.

Gordon, Robert. *1 & 2 Samuel: A Commentary*. Grand Rapids: Zondervan, 1986. One-to-one, detailed, evangelical.

Hertzberg, H. W. *1 Samuel*. OTL. Philadelphia: Westminster Press, 1964. One-to-one, detailed, technical, liberal.

Keil, C. F., and Delitzsch, F. *The Books of Samuel*. K-D. Repr. Grand Rapids: Eerdmans, 1988. One-to-one, in-depth, technical, evangelical.

Klein, Ralph W. *1 Samuel*. WBC. Waco, TX: Word Books, 1983. One-to-one, in-depth, technical, liberal.

Mauchline, J. *1 and 2 Samuel*. NCB. London: Oliphants, 1971. One-to-one, detailed, serious, liberal.

McCarter, P. Kyle. *I Samuel*. AB. Garden City: Doubleday, 1980. One-to-one, in-depth, technical, liberal.

McKane, W. *I and II Samuel: The Way to the Throne*. TBC. London: SCM, 1963. One-to-one, semi-detailed, technical, liberal.

Payne, D. F. *Samuel*. DSB. Philadelphia: Westminster Press, 1982. One-to-one, semi-detailed, popular, liberal.

Smith, H. P. *A Critical and Exegetical Commentary on the Books of Samuel*. ICC. Edinburgh: T. & T. Clark, 1899. One-to-one, in-depth, technical, liberal.

Vos, Howard. *1, 2 Samuel*. BSC. Grand Rapids: Zondervan, 1986. One-to-one, semi-detailed, popular, evangelical.

2 Samuel

Ackroyd, Peter R. *The Second Book of Samuel*. CBCNEB. Cambridge and New York: Cambridge University Press, 1977. One-to-one, detailed, serious, liberal.

Anderson, A. A. *2 Samuel*. WBC. Waco, TX: Word Books, 1989. One-to-one, in-depth, technical, conservative-moderate.

Baldwin, Joyce: see 1 Samuel.

Caird, G. B.: see 1 Samuel.

Conroy, Charles: see 1 Samuel.

Goldman, S.: see 1 Samuel.

Gordon, Robert: see 1 Samuel.

Keil, C. F., and Delitzsch, F.: see 1 Samuel.

Mauchline, J.: see 1 Samuel.

McCarter, P. Kyle. *II Samuel*. AB. Garden City: Doubleday, 1984. One-to-one, in-depth, technical, liberal.

McKane, W.: see 1 Samuel.

Payne, D. F.: see 1 Samuel

Smith, H. P.: see 1 Samuel.

Vos, Howard: see 1 Samuel.

1 Kings

Conroy, Charles: see 1 Samuel.

DeVries, Simon J. *1 Kings*. WBC. Waco, TX: Word Books, 1985. One-to-one, in-depth, technical, liberal.

Gray, John. *1 and 2 Kings*. 2d ed. OTL. Philadelphia: Westminster Press, 1970. One-to-one, in-depth, technical, liberal.

Jones, G. H. *1 Kings*. NCBC. Grand Rapids: Eerdmans, 1984. One-to-one, in-depth, technical, liberal.

Keil, C. F. *The Books of the Kings*. K-D. Repr. Grand Rapids: Eerdmans, 1988. One-to-one, in-depth, technical, evangelical.

Montgomery, John A., and Gehman, H. S. *A Critical and Exegetical Commentary on the Books of Kings*. ICC. Edinburgh: T. & T. Clark, 1951. One-to-one, in-depth, technical, liberal.

Nelson, Richard. *First and Second Kings*. INT. Atlanta: John Knox, 1987. One-to-one, detailed, serious, liberal.

Patterson, Richard D., and Austel, Herman J. *1 and 2 Kings*. EBC. Grand Rapids: Zondervan, 1988. One-to-several, detailed, serious, evangelical.

Robinson, J. *The First Book of Kings*. CBCNEB. Cambridge: Cambridge University Press, 1972. One-to-one, semi-detailed, serious, liberal.

Snaith, Norman. *I and II Kings*. IB. Nashville: Abingdon, 1952. One-to-several, semi-detailed, technical, liberal.

Vos, Howard. *1, 2 Kings*. BSC. Grand Rapids: Zondervan, 1989. One-to-one, semi-detailed, popular, evangelical.

Wifall, W. *The Court History of Israel: A Commentary on First and Second Kings*. St. Louis: Clayton Publishing House, 1975. One-to-one, detailed, technical, liberal.

2 Kings

Conroy, Charles: see 1 Samuel.

Gray, John: see 1 Kings.

Hobbs, T. R. *2 Kings*. WBC. Waco, TX: Word Books, 1985. One-to-one, in-depth, technical, conservative-moderate.

Jones, G. H. *2 Kings*. NCBC. Grand Rapids: Eerdmans, 1984. One-to-one, in-depth, technical, liberal.

Keil, C. F.: see 1 Kings.

Montgomery, J. A., and Gehman, H. S.: see 1 Kings.

Nelson, Richard: see 1 Kings.

Patterson, Richard, and Austel, Herman: see 1 Kings.

Robinson, J. *The Second Book of Kings*. CBCNEB. Cambridge: Cambridge University Press, 1976. One-to-one, semi-detailed, serious, liberal.

Snaith, Norman: see 1 Kings.

Vos, Howard: see 1 Kings.

Wifall, W.: see 1 Kings.

1 Chronicles

Ackroyd, Peter. *I and II Chronicles, Ezra, Nehemiah*. TBC. London: SCM, 1973. One-to-one, semi-detailed, serious, liberal.

Braun, Roddy. *1 Chronicles.* WBC. Waco, TX: Word Books, 1986. One-to-one, in-depth, technical, liberal.

Coggins, R. J. *The First and Second Books of Chronicles.* CBCNEB. Cambridge: Cambridge University Press, 1976. One-to-one, semi-detailed, technical, liberal.

Curtis, E. L., and Madsen, A. A. *A Critical and Exegetical Commentary on the Books of Chronicles.* ICC. Edinburgh: T. & T. Clark, 1910. One-to-one, in-depth, technical, liberal.

Elmslie, W. A. L. *I and II Chronicles.* IB. Nashville: Abingdon, 1952. One-to-several, semi-detailed, technical, liberal.

Keil, C. F. *The Books of the Chronicles.* K-D. Repr. Grand Rapids: Eerdmans, 1988. One-to-one, in-depth, technical, evangelical.

Mangan, Celine, OP. *1–2 Chronicles, Ezra, Nehemiah.* OTM. Wilmington, DE: Michael Glazier, 1982. One-to-several, summary, serious, liberal.

McConville, J. *I and II Chronicles.* DSB. Philadelphia: Westminster, 1984. One-to-one, semi-detailed, popular, liberal.

Merrill, Eugene. *1, 2 Chronicles.* BSC. Grand Rapids: Zondervan, 1988. One-to-one, semi-detailed, popular, evangelical.

Myers, Jacob. *I Chronicles.* AB. Garden City: Doubleday, 1965. One-to-one, semi-detailed, technical, liberal.

Payne, J. Barton. *1 and 2 Chronicles.* EBC. Grand Rapids: Zondervan, 1988. One-to-several, detailed, serious, evangelical.

Sailhamer, John. *1 and 2 Chronicles.* Everyman's Bible Commentary. Chicago: Moody Press, 1983. One-to-one, semi-detailed, popular, evangelical.

Slotki, I. W. *Chronicles.* Soncino Books of the Bible. London: Soncino Press, 1952. One-to-one, detailed, technical, liberal.

Wilcock, Michael. *The Message of Chronicles.* TBST. Leicester, England; Downers Grove, IL: InterVarsity, 1982. One-to-one, semi-detailed, serious, evangelical.

Williamson, H. G. M. *1 and 2 Chronicles.* NCBC. Grand Rapids: Eerdmans, 1982. One-to-one, semi-detailed, technical, liberal.

2 Chronicles

Ackroyd, Peter: see 1 Chronicles.

Coggins, R. J.: see 1 Chronicles

Curtis, E. L., and Madsen, A. A.: see 1 Chronicles.

Dillard, Raymond B. *2 Chronicles.* WBC. Waco, TX: Word Books, 1987. One-to-one, in-depth, technical, conservative-moderate.

Elmslie, W. A. L.: see 1 Chronicles.

Keil, C. F.: see 1 Chronicles.
Mangan, Celine: see 1 Chronicles.
McConville, J.: see 1 Chronicles.
Merrill, Eugene: see 1 Chronicles.
Myers, Jacob. *II Chronicles*. AB. Garden City: Doubleday, 1965.
  One-to-one, semi-detailed, technical, liberal.
Payne, J. Barton: see 1 Chronicles.
Sailhamer, John: see 1 Chronicles.
Slotki, I. W.: see 1 Chronicles.
Wilcock, Michael: see 1 Chronicles.
Williamson, H. G. M.: see 1 Chronicles.

Ezra

Ackroyd, Peter: see 1 Chronicles.
Batten, L. W. *A Critical and Exegetical Commentary on Books of Ezra
  and Nehemiah*. ICC. Edinburgh: T. & T. Clark, 1913. One-to-
  one, in-depth, technical, liberal.
Blenskinsopp, Joseph. *Ezra-Nehemiah, A Commentary*. OTL. Louis-
  ville: Westminster/John Knox, 1988. One-to-one, in-depth,
  technical, liberal.
Bowman, Raymond A. *Ezra: Introduction and Exegesis*. IB.
  Nashville: Abingdon, 1952. One-to-several, semi-detailed,
  technical, liberal.
Brockington, L. H. *Ezra, Nehemiah, and Esther*. NCBC. London:
  Thomas Nelson, 1969. One-to-one, semi-detailed, serious,
  liberal.
Clines, D. J. *Ezra, Nehemiah, Esther*. NCBC. Grand Rapids: Eerd-
  mans, 1984. One-to-one, detailed, serious, liberal.
Fensham, F. Charles. *The Books of Ezra and Nehemiah*. NICOT.
  Grand Rapids: Eerdmans, 1982. One-to one, in-depth, techni-
  cal, evangelical.
Keil, C. F. *The Book of Ezra*. K-D. Repr. Grand Rapids: Eerdmans,
  1988. One-to-one, in-depth, technical, evangelical.
Kidner, Derek. *Ezra and Nehemiah*. TOTC. Downers Grove, IL:
  InterVarsity, 1979. One-to-one, detailed, serious, evangelical.
Mangan, Celine: see 1 Chronicles.
Myers, Jacob. *Ezra. Nehemiah*. AB. Garden City: Doubleday, 1965.
  One-to-one, semi-detailed, technical, liberal.
Slotki, J. J.: see Daniel.
Vos, Howard. *Ezra, Nehemiah, Esther*. BSC. Grand Rapids: Zonder-
  van, 1987. One-to-one, semi-detailed, popular, evangelical.

Williamson, H. G. M. *Ezra, Nehemiah.* WBC. Waco, TX: Word Books, 1985. One-to-one, in-depth, technical, conservative-moderate.

Yamauchi, Edwin. *Ezra and Nehemiah.* EBC. Grand Rapids: Zondervan, 1988. One-to-several, detailed, serious, evangelical.

Nehemiah

Ackroyd, Peter: see 1 Chronicles.

Batten, L. W.: see Ezra.

Blenkinsopp, Joseph: see Ezra.

Bowman, Raymond A. *Nehemiah: Introduction and Exegesis.* IB. Nashville: Abingdon, 1952. One-to-several, semi-detailed, technical, liberal.

Brockington, L. H.: see Ezra.

Clines, D. J.: see Ezra.

Fensham, F. Charles: see Ezra.

Keil, C. F. *The Book of Nehemiah.* K-D. Repr. Grand Rapids: Eerdmans, 1988. One-to-one, in-depth, technical, evangelical.

Kidner, Derek: see Ezra.

Mangan, Cecile: see 1 Chronicles.

Myers, Jacob: see Ezra.

Slotki, J. J.: see Daniel.

Vos, Howard: see Ezra.

Williamson, H. G. M.: see Ezra.

Yamauchi, Edwin: see Ezra.

Esther

Anderson, Bernhard. *Esther.* IB. Nashville: Abingdon, 1952. One-to-several, semi-detailed, technical, liberal.

Baldwin, Joyce. *Esther.* TOTC. Downers Grove, IL: InterVarsity, 1984. One-to-one, detailed, serious, evangelical.

Brockington, L. H.: see Ezra.

Clines, D. J.: see Ezra.

Coggins, R. J., and Re'emi, S. P.: see Nahum.

Craghan, John. *Esther, Judith, Tobit, Jonah, Ruth.* OTM. Wilmington, DE: Michael Glazier, 1982. One-to-several, summary, serious, liberal.

Huey, F. B., Jr. *Esther.* EBC. Grand Rapids: Zondervan, 1988. One-to-several, detailed, serious, evangelical.

Keil, C. F. *The Book of Esther.* K-D. Repr. Grand Rapids: Eerdmans, 1988. One-to-one, in-depth, technical, evangelical.

Knight, G. A. F. *Esther, Song of Songs, Lamentations.* New York: Macmillan, 1955. One-to-one, detailed, serious, liberal.

Moore, Carey A. *Esther.* AB. Garden City: Doubleday, 1971. One-to-one, detailed, technical, liberal.

Paton, L. B. *Esther.* ICC. Edinburgh: T. & T. Clark, 1908. One-to-one, in-depth, technical, liberal.

Vos, Howard: see Ezra.

Job

Anderson, Francis. *Job.* TOTC. Downers Grove, IL: InterVarsity, 1976. One-to-one, detailed, serious, evangelical.

Bergant, Dianne, CSA. *Job, Ecclesiastes.* OTM. Wilmington, DE: Michael Glazier, 1982. One-to-several, semi-detailed, serious, liberal.

Clines, David J. A. *Job 1–20.* WBC. Waco, TX: Word Books, 1989. One-to-one, in-depth, technical, liberal.

Delitzsch, Franz. *The Book of Job.* 2 vols. K-D. Repr. Grand Rapids: Eerdmans, 1988. One-to-one, in-depth, technical, evangelical.

Dhorme, E. *A Commentary on the Book of Job.* London: Thomas Nelson, 1967 (orig. 1926). One-to-one, in-depth, technical, liberal.

Driver, S. R. and Gray, George Buchanan. *A Critical and Exegetical Commentary on the Book of Job.* ICC. Edinburgh: T. & T. Clark, 1921. One-to-one, in-depth, technical, liberal.

Ellison, H. L. *A Study of Job: From Tragedy to Triumph.* Grand Rapids: Zondervan, 1971. One-to-one, semi-detailed, serious, evangelical.

Garland, D. David. *Job.* BSC. Grand Rapids: Zondervan, 1971. One-to-one, semi-detailed, popular, evangelical.

Gibson, J. C. L. *Job.* DSB. Philadelphia: Westminster, 1985. One-to-one, summary, popular, liberal.

Gordis, Robert. *The Book of Job: Commentary, New Translation, and Special Notes.* New York: Jewish Theological Seminary, 1978. One-to-one, in-depth, technical, liberal.

Habel, Norman. *The Book of Job, A Commentary.* OTL. Louisville: Westminster/John Knox, 1985. One-to-one, in-depth, technical, conservative-moderate.

————. *The Book of Job.* CBCNEB. Cambridge: Cambridge University Press, 1975. One-to-one, semi-detailed, serious, conservative-moderate.

Hartley, John E. *The Book of Job.* NICOT. Grand Rapids: Eerdmans, 1988. One-to one, in-depth, technical, evangelical.

Janzen, J. Gerald. *Job.* INT. Atlanta: John Knox, 1985. One-to-one, detailed, serious, liberal.

Kissane, E. J. *The Book of Job.* Dublin: Browne and Nolan, 1939. One-to-one, detailed, serious, conservative-moderate.

Pope, Marvin H. *Job.* 3d ed. AB. Garden City: Doubleday, 1973. One-to-one, semi-detailed, technical, liberal.

Rowley, H. H. *Job.* NCBC. Grand Rapids: Eerdmans, 1970. One-to-one, detailed, technical, liberal.

Selms, A. van. *Job.* TAI. Grand Rapids: Eerdmans, 1985. One-to-one, summary, serious, liberal.

Smick, Elmer. *Job.* EBC. Grand Rapids: Zondervan, 1988. One-to-several, detailed, technical, evangelical.

Terrien, Samuel. *Job: Introduction and Exegesis.* IB. Nashville: Abingdon, 1952. One-to-several, semi-detailed, technical, liberal.

Torczyner (Tur-Sinai), Harry. *The Book of Job: A New Commentary.* Jerusalem: Kiryath Sepher, 1957. One-to-one, detailed, technical, liberal.

Psalms

Allen, Leslie C. *Psalms 101–150.* WBC. Waco, TX: Word Books, 1983. One-to-one, in-depth, technical, conservative-moderate.

Anderson, A. A. *Psalms 1–72.* NCBC. Grand Rapids: Eerdmans, 1972. One-to-one, in-depth, technical, liberal.

————. *Psalms 73–150.* NCBC. Grand Rapids: Eerdmans, 1972. One-to-one, in-depth, technical, liberal.

Briggs, C. A., and Briggs, E. G. *A Critical and Exegetical Commentary on the Book of Psalms.* 2 vols. ICC. Edinburgh: T. & T. Clark, 1906. One-to-one, in-depth, technical, liberal.

Craigie, Peter. *Psalms 1–50.* WBC. Waco, TX: Word Books, 1983. One-to-one, in-depth, technical, evangelical.

Dahood, Mitchell. *Psalms I. 1–50.* AB. Garden City: Doubleday, 1966. One-to-one, detailed, technical, conservative-moderate.

————. *Psalms II. 51–100.* AB. Garden City: Doubleday, 1968. One-to-one, detailed, technical, conservative-moderate.

———. *Psalms III. 101–150.* AB. Garden City: Doubleday, 1970. One-to-one, detailed, technical, conservative-moderate.

Delitzsch, Franz. *The Psalms.* 3 vols. K-D. Repr. Grand Rapids: Eerdmans, 1988. One-to-one, in-depth, technical, evangelical.

Durham, J. I. *Commentary on Psalms.* The Broadman Bible Commentary. Nashville: Broadman Press, 1972. One-to-one, semi-detailed, serious, conservative-moderate.

Eaton, J. H. *Psalms.* TBC. London: SCM, 1967. One-to-one, semi-detailed, serious, liberal.

Kidner, Derek. *Psalms 1–72.* TOTC. Downers Grove, IL: InterVarsity, 1973. One-to-one, semi-detailed, serious, evangelical.

———. *Psalms 73–150.* TOTC. Downers Grove, IL: InterVarsity, 1975. One-to-one, semi-detailed, serious, evangelical.

Kissane, E. J. *The Book of Psalms.* 2 vols. Dublin: Browne and Nolan, 1953, 1954. One-to-one, detailed, serious, conservative-moderate.

Kraus, Hans-Joachim. *Psalms 1–59.* CC. Minneapolis: Augsburg, 1987. One-to-one, in-depth, technical, liberal.

———. *Psalms 60–150.* CC. Minneapolis: Augsburg Fortress, 1989. One-to-one, in-depth, technical, liberal.

Leupold, Herbert C. *Exposition of Psalms.* Grand Rapids: Baker, 1972. One-to-one, semi-detailed, serious, evangelical.

Oesterly, W. O. E. *The Psalms.* 2 vols. London: SPCK, 1939. One-to-one, detailed, technical, liberal.

Rogerson, J. W., and McKay, J. W. *Psalms 1–50.* CBCNEB. Cambridge: Cambridge University Press, 1977. One-to-one, semi-detailed, serious, liberal.

Stuhlmueller, Carroll. *Psalms 1.* OTM. Wilmington, DE: Michael Glazier, 1983. One-to-one, semi-detailed, serious, liberal.

———. *Psalms 2.* OTM. Wilmington, DE: Michael Glazier, 1983. One-to-one, semi-detailed, serious, liberal.

Taylor, William. *Psalms.* IB. Nashville: Abingdon, 1952. One-to-several, semi-detailed, technical, liberal.

VanGemeren, Willem A. *Psalms.* EBC. Grand Rapids: Zondervan, 1989. One-to-several, detailed, serious, evangelical.

Weiser, Artur. *The Psalms, A Commentary.* OTL. Philadelphia: Westminster, 1962. One-to-one, detailed, technical, liberal.

Proverbs

Alden, Robert L. *Proverbs. A Commentary on an Ancient Book of Timeless Advice.* Grand Rapids: Baker, 1989. One-to-one, semi-detailed, serious, evangelical.

Cox, Dermot, OFM. *Proverbs, with Introduction to Sapiential Books.* OTM. Wilmington, DE: Michael Glazier, 1982. One-to-one, summary, serious, liberal.

Delitzsch, F. *The Book of Proverbs.* 2 vols. K-D. Repr. Grand Rapids: Eerdmans, 1988. One-to-one, in-depth, technical, evangelical.

Fritsch, Charles. *Proverbs.* IB. Nashville: Abingdon, 1952. One-to-several, semi-detailed, technical, liberal.

Johnson, L. D. *Proverbs, Ecclesiastes, Song of Solomon.* Layman's Bible Book Commentary. Nashville: Broadman Press, 1982. One-to-one, semi-detailed, popular, conservative-moderate.

Jones, D. R. *Proverbs and Ecclesiastes.* TBC. London: SCM, 1961. One-to-one, semi-detailed, popular, liberal.

Kidner, Derek. *Proverbs.* TOTC. Downers Grove, IL: InterVarsity, 1975. One-to-one, semi-detailed, serious, evangelical.

McKane, W. *Proverbs.* OTL. Philadelphia: Westminster, 1970. One-to-one, in-depth, technical, liberal.

Ross, Allen P. *Proverbs.* EBC. Grand Rapids: Zondervan, 1989. One-to-several, semi-detailed, serious, evangelical.

Rylaarsdam, J. C. *Proverbs, Ecclesiastes, Song of Solomon.* LBC. Philadelphia: Westminster, 1965. One-to-one, semi-detailed, popular, liberal.

Scott, R. B. Y. *Proverbs, Ecclesiastes.* AB. Garden City: Doubleday, 1965. One-to-one, semi-detailed, technical, liberal.

Toy, Crawford H. *Proverbs.* ICC. Edinburgh: T. & T. Clark, 1899. One-to-one, in-depth, technical, liberal.

Whybray, R. N. *Proverbs.* CBCNEB. Cambridge: Cambridge University Press, 1972. One-to-one, semi-detailed, serious, liberal.

Woodcock, Eldon. *Proverbs.* BSC. Grand Rapids: Zondervan, 1988. One-to-one, detailed, popular, evangelical.

Ecclesiastes

Barton, G. A. *A Critical and Exegetical Commentary on the Book of Ecclesiastes.* ICC. Edinburgh: T. & T. Clark, 1908. One-to-one, in-depth, technical, liberal.

Bergant, Dianne: see Job.

Crenshaw, James. *Ecclesiastes, A Commentary.* OTL. Philadelphia: Westminster, 1987. One-to-one, in-depth, technical, liberal.

Davidson, R. *Ecclesiastes and Song of Solomon.* DSB. Philadelphia: Westminster, 1986.

Delitzsch, F. *The Book of Ecclesiastes.* K-D. Repr. Grand Rapids: Eerdmans, 1988. One-to-one, in-depth, technical, evangelical.

Eaton, Michael. *Ecclesiastes.* TOTC. Downers Grove, IL: InterVarsity, 1983. One-to-one, detailed, serious, evangelical.

Fuerst, W. J.: see Ruth.

Goldberg, Louis. *Ecclesiastes.* BSC. Grand Rapids: Zondervan, 1986. One-to-one, semi-detailed, popular, evangelical.

Gordis, Robert. *Koheleth: The Man and His World.* 3d ed. New York: Schocken, 1968. One-to-one, in-depth, technical, liberal.

Johnson, L. D.: see Proverbs.

Jones, D. R.: see Proverbs.

Kidner, Derek. *A Time to Mourn and a Time to Dance: Ecclesiastes and the Way of the World.* Downers Grove, Ill: InterVarsity, 1976. One-to-one, detailed, serious, evangelical.

———. *The Message of Ecclesiastes.* TBST. Downers Grove, IL: InterVarsity, 1988. One-to-one, semi-detailed, serious, evangelical.

Leupold, Herbert C. *Exposition of Ecclesiastes.* Grand Rapids: Baker, 1966. One-to-one, semi-detailed, serious, evangelical.

Loader, J. A. *Ecclesiastes.* TAI. Grand Rapids: Eerdmans, 1986. One-to-one, summary, serious, liberal.

Rankin, O. S. *Ecclesiastes: Introduction and Exegesis.* IB. Nashville: Abingdon, 1952. One-to-several, semi-detailed, technical, liberal.

Rylaarsdam, J. C.: see Proverbs.

Scott, R. B. Y.: see Proverbs.

Whybray, R. N. *Ecclesiastes.* NCBC. Grand Rapids: Eerdmans, 1989. One-to-one, in-depth, technical, liberal.

Wright, J. Stafford. *Ecclesiastes.* EBC. Grand Rapids: Zondervan, 1989. One-to-several, detailed, serious, evangelical.

Song of Songs

Carr, G. Lloyd. *The Song of Solomon.* TOTC. Downers Grove, IL: InterVarsity, 1984. One-to-one, detailed, serious, evangelical.

Curtis, Edward. *Song of Songs.* BSC. Grand Rapids: Zondervan, 1988. One-to-one, semi-detailed, popular, evangelical.

Davidson, R.: see Ecclesiastes.
Delitzsch, F. *The Song of Songs.* K-D. Repr. Grand Rapids: Eerdmans, 1988. One-to-one, in-depth, technical, evangelical.
Fuerst, W. J.: see Ruth.
Gordis, Robert. *The Song of Songs and Lamentations.* Rev. ed. New York: Ktav, 1974. One-to-one, in-depth, technical, liberal.
Johnson, L. D.: see Proverbs.
Kinlaw, Dennis F. *Song of Songs.* EBC. Grand Rapids: Zondervan, 1989. One-to-several, detailed, serious, evangelical.
Knight, G. A. F.: see Esther.
Meek, Theophile. *Song of Songs: Introduction and Exegesis.* IB. Nashville: Abingdon, 1952. One-to-several, semi-detailed, technical, liberal.
Murphy, Roland, O. Carm. *The Song of Songs.* HERM. Philadelphia: Fortress, 1990. One-to-one, in-depth, technical, liberal.
Pope, Marvin H. *Song of Songs.* AB. Garden City: Doubleday, 1977. One-to-one, in-depth, technical, liberal.
Reese, James, OSFS. *The Book of Wisdom, Song of Songs.* OTM. Wilmington, DE: Michael Glazier, 1982. One-to-several, semi-detailed, serious, liberal.
Rylaarsdam, J. C.: see Proverbs.

Isaiah

Butler, Trent C. *Isaiah.* Layman's Bible Book Commentary. Nashville: Broadman Press, 1982. One-to-one, semi-detailed, popular, conservative-moderate.
Clements, Ronald E. *Isaiah 1–39.* NCBC. Grand Rapids: Eerdmans, 1980. One-to-one, detailed, serious, liberal.
Delitzsch, F. *The Prophecies of Isaiah.* 2 vols. K-D. Repr. Grand Rapids: Eerdmans, 1988. One-to-one, in-depth, technical, evangelical.
Garland, D. David. *Isaiah.* BSC. Grand Rapids: Zondervan, 1968. One-to-one, semi-detailed, popular, evangelical.
Gray, George Buchanan. *A Critical and Exegetical Commentary on the Book of Isaiah I–XXVI.* ICC. Edinburgh: T. & T. Clark, 1912. One-to-one, in-depth, technical, liberal.
Grogan, Geoffrey. *Isaiah.* EBC. Grand Rapids: Zondervan, 1986. One-to-several, detailed, serious, evangelical.
Herbert, A. S. *The Book of the Prophet Isaiah. Chapters 1–39.* CBC-NEB. Cambridge: Cambridge University Press, 1973. One-to-one, summary, serious, liberal.

Jensen, Joseph, OSB. *Isaiah 1–39*. OTM. Wilmington, DE: Michael Glazier, 1984. One-to-one, semi-detailed, serious, liberal.

Jones, D. R. *Isaiah 55–66 and Joel*. TBC. London: SCM, 1964. One-to-one, semi-detailed, serious, liberal.

Kaiser, Otto. *Isaiah 1–12, A Commentary*. 2d ed. OTL. Philadelphia: Westminster, 1983. One-to-one, in-depth, technical, liberal.

———. *Isaiah 13–39, A Commentary*. 2d ed. OTL. Philadelphia: Westminster, 1983. One-to-one, in-depth, technical, liberal.

Kissane, E. J. *The Book of Isaiah*. 2 vols. Rev. ed. Dublin: Browne and Nolan, 1960. One-to-one, detailed, serious, conservative-moderate.

Knight, G. A. F. *Deutero–Isaiah*. Nashville: Abingdon, 1965. One-to-one, semi-detailed, serious, liberal.

Leslie, E. A. *Isaiah*. Nashville: Abingdon, 1963. One-to-one, detailed, serious, liberal.

Leupold, Herbert C. *Exposition of Isaiah*. Grand Rapids: Baker, 1968. One-to-one, semi-detailed, serious, evangelical.

Mauchline, J. *Isaiah 1–39*. TBC. London: SCM, 1962. One-to-one, semi-detailed, serious, liberal.

McKenzie, J. L. *Second Isaiah*. AB. Garden City, NY: Doubleday, 1968. One-to-one, semi-detailed, serious, liberal.

Muilenburg, James. *Isaiah 40–66: Introduction and Exegesis*. IB. Nashville: Abingdon, 1952. One-to-several, semi-detailed, technical, liberal.

North, C. R. *Isaiah 40–55*. TBC. London: SCM, 1952. One-to-one, semi-detailed, serious, liberal.

———. *The Second Isaiah*. Oxford: Oxford University Press, 1964. One-to-one, detailed, technical, liberal.

Oswalt, John. *The Book of Isaiah, Chapters 1–39*. NICOT. Grand Rapids: Eerdmans, 1986. One-to-one, in-depth, technical, evangelical.

Ridderbos, J. *Isaiah*. BSC. Grand Rapids: Zondervan, 1985. One-to-one, detailed, serious, evangelical.

Scott, R. B. Y. *Isaiah 1–39: Introduction and Exegesis*. IB. Nashville: Abingdon, 1952. One-to-several, semi-detailed, technical, liberal.

Scullion, John, SJ. *Isaiah 40–66*. OTM. Wilmington, DE: Michael Glazier, 1982. One-to-one, semi-detailed, serious, liberal.

Smart, James D. *History and Theology in Second Isaiah*. Philadelphia: Westminster, 1965. One-to-one, semi-detailed, technical, liberal.

Watts, John D. W. *Isaiah 1–33*. WBC. Waco, TX: Word Books, 1985. One-to-one, in-depth, technical, conservative-moderate.
———. *Isaiah 34–66*. WBC. Waco, TX: Word Books, 1987. One-to-one, in-depth, technical, conservative-moderate.
Westermann, Claus. *Isaiah 40–66, A Commentary*. OTL. Philadelphia: Westminster, 1969. One-to-one, in-depth, technical, liberal.
Whybray, R. N. *Isaiah 40–66*. NCBC. Grand Rapids: Eerdmans, 1975. One-to-one, detailed, technical, liberal.
Wolf, Herbert. *Interpreting Isaiah: The Suffering and Glory of the Messiah*. Grand Rapids: Zondervan, 1985. One-to-one, detailed, serious, evangelical.
Young, E. J. *The Book of Isaiah*. 3 vols. NICOT. Grand Rapids: Eerdmans, 1965–72. One-to-one, in-depth, technical, evangelical.

Jeremiah

Achtemeier, Elizabeth: see Deuteronomy.
Boadt, Lawrence, CSP. *Jeremiah 1–25*. OTM. Wilmington, DE: Michael Glazier, 1982. One-to-one, semi-detailed, serious, liberal.
———. *Jeremiah 26–52, Habakkuk, Zephaniah, Nahum*. OTM. Wilmington, DE: Michael Glazier, 1982. One-to-one, semi-detailed, serious, liberal.
Bright, John. *Jeremiah*. AB. Garden City: Doubleday, 1965. One-to-one, semi-detailed, technical, liberal.
Carroll, Robert. *Jeremiah, A Commentary*. OTL. Philadelphia: Westminster, 1986. One-to-one, in-depth, technical, liberal.
Clements, R. E. *Jeremiah*. INT. Louisville: Westminster/John Knox, 1989. One-to-one, semi-detailed, serious, liberal.
Cunliffe-Jones H. *The Book of Jeremiah*. TBC. London: SCM, 1960. One-to-one, semi-detailed, serious, liberal.
Feinberg, Charles. *Jeremiah*. EBC. Grand Rapids: Zondervan, 1986. One-to-several, detailed, serious, evangelical.
———. *Jeremiah: A Commentary*. Grand Rapids: Zondervan, 1982. One-to-one, detailed, serious, evangelical.
Freedman, H. *Jeremiah*. Soncino Books of the Bible. London: Soncino Press, 1949. One-to-one, detailed, serious, liberal.
Harrison, R. K. *Jeremiah and Lamentations*. TOTC. Downers Grove, IL: InterVarsity, 1973. One-to-one, detailed, serious, evangelical.

Holladay, William L. *Jeremiah 1.* (Chs. 1–25) HERM. Philadelphia: Fortress, 1986. One-to-one, in-depth, technical, liberal.
———. *Jeremiah 2.* (Chs. 26–52). HERM. Philadelphia: Fortress, 1989. One-to-one, in-depth, technical, liberal.
Huey, F. B., Jr. *Jeremiah.* BSC. Grand Rapids: Zondervan, 1981. One-to-one, semi-detailed, popular, evangelical.
Hyatt, James Philip. *Jeremiah.* IB. Nashville: Abingdon, 1952. One-to-several, semi-detailed, technical, liberal.
Keil, C. F. *The Prophecies of Jeremiah.* 2 vols. K-D. Repr. Grand Rapids: Eerdmans, 1988. One-to-one, in-depth, technical, evangelical.
Kidner, Derek, and Motyer, J. A. *The Message of Jeremiah.* TBST. Leicester, England; Downers Grove, IL: InterVarsity, 1987. One-to-one, semi-detailed, serious, evangelical.
Laetsch, T. *Jeremiah.* St. Louis: Concordia, 1952. One-to-one, in-depth, serious, evangelical.
Leslie, E. A. *Jeremiah.* Nashville: Abingdon, 1954. One-to-one, detailed, serious, liberal.
McKane, William. *A Critical and Exegetical Commentary on the Book of Jeremiah.* Vol. 1 (Jer 1–25) only. ICC. Edinburgh: T. & T. Clark, 1986. One-to-one, in-depth, technical, liberal.
Nicholson, Ernest W. *The Book of the Prophet Jeremiah Chapters 1–25.* CBCNEB. Cambridge: Cambridge University Press, 1973. One-to-one, summary, serious, liberal.
———. *The Book of the Prophet Jeremiah Chapters 26–52.* CBCNEB. Cambridge: Cambridge University Press, 1975. One-to-one, summary, serious, liberal.
Thompson, J. A. *The Book of Jeremiah.* NICOT. Grand Rapids: Eerdmans, 1980. One-to-one, in-depth, technical, evangelical.

Lamentations

Ellison, H. L. *Lamentations.* EBC. Grand Rapids: Zondervan, 1986. One-to-several, detailed, serious, evangelical.
Harrison, R. K.: see Jeremiah.
Hillers, Delbert. *Lamentations.* AB. Garden City: Doubleday, 1973. One-to-one, detailed, technical, liberal.
Keil, C. F. *The Lamentations.* K-D. Repr. Grand Rapids: Eerdmans, 1988. One-to-one, in-depth, technical, evangelical.
Kent, Dan. *Lamentations.* BSC. Grand Rapids: Zondervan, 1983. One-to-one, semi-detailed, popular, evangelical.

Knight, G. A. F.: see Esther.
Kodell, Jerome, OSB. *Lamentations, Haggai, Zechariah, Second Zechariah, Malachi, Obadiah, Joel, Baruch.* OTM. Wilmington, DE: Michael Glazier, 1982. One-to-several, summary, serious, liberal.
Meek, Theophile. *Lamentations.* IB. Nashville: Abingdon, 1952. One-to-several, semi-detailed, technical, liberal.

Ezekiel

Alexander, Ralph. *Ezekiel.* EBC. Grand Rapids: Zondervan, 1986. One-to-several, detailed, serious, evangelical.
Carley, K. W. *The Book of the Prophet Ezekiel.* CBCNEB. Cambridge: Cambridge University Press, 1974. One-to-one, semi-detailed, serious, liberal.
Cody, Aelred, OSB. *Ezekiel, with Excursus on Old Testament Priesthood.* OTM. Wilmington, DE: Michael Glazier, 1984. One-to-one, semi-detailed, serious, liberal.
Cooke, G. A. *A Critical and Exegetical Commentary on the Book of Ezekiel.* ICC. Edinburgh: T. & T. Clark, 1936. One-to-one, in-depth, technical, liberal.
Craigie, Peter C. *Ezekiel.* DSB. Philadelphia: Westminster, 1983. One-to-one, semi-detailed, popular, evangelical.
Eichrodt, Walther. *Ezekiel, A Commentary.* OTL. Philadelphia: Westminster, 1970. One-to-one, in-depth, technical, liberal.
Enns, Paul. *Ezekiel.* BSC. Grand Rapids: Zondervan, 1986. One-to-one, detailed, popular, evangelical.
Greenberg, Moshe. *Ezekiel I–XX.* AB. Garden City: Doubleday, 1983. One-to-one, detailed, technical, liberal.
Howie, C. G. *The Book of Ezekiel. The Book of Daniel.* LBC. Atlanta: John Knox, 1961. One-to-one, semi-detailed, popular, liberal.
Keil, C. F. *The Prophecies of Ezekiel.* 2 vols. K-D. Repr. Grand Rapids: Eerdmans, 1988. One-to-one, in-depth, technical, evangelical.
May, Herbert. *Ezekiel: Introduction and Exegesis.* IB. Nashville: Abingdon, 1952. One-to-several, semi-detailed, technical, liberal.
Smith, J. *The Book of the Prophet Ezekiel.* New York: Macmillan, 1931. One-to-one, semi-detailed, serious, liberal.
Stuart, Douglas. *Ezekiel.* Dallas: Word Books, 1989. One-to-one, detailed, popular, evangelical.
Taylor, John. *Ezekiel.* TOTC. Downers Grove, IL: InterVarsity, 1969. One-to-one, detailed, serious, evangelical.

Wevers, John W. *Ezekiel.* NCBC. Grand Rapids: Eerdmans, 1969. One-to-one, semi-detailed, technical, liberal.

Zimmerli, Walther. *Ezekiel 1.* (Chs. 1–24) HERM. Philadelphia: Fortress, 1979. One-to-one, in-depth, technical, liberal.

————. *Ezekiel 2.* (Chs. 25–48) HERM. Philadelphia: Fortress, 1983. One-to-one, in-depth, technical, liberal.

Daniel

Anderson, R. A. *Signs and Wonders: A Commentary on the Book of Daniel.* ITC. Grand Rapids: Eerdmans, 1984. One-to-one, detailed, serious, liberal.

Archer, Gleason, Jr. *Daniel.* EBC. Grand Rapids: Zondervan, 1985. One-to-several, detailed, serious, evangelical.

Baldwin, Joyce. *Daniel.* TOTC. Downers Grove, IL: InterVarsity, 1978. One-to-one, detailed, serious, evangelical.

Charles, R. H. *A Critical and Exegetical Commentary on the Book of Daniel.* Oxford: Clarendon Press, 1929. One-to-one, in-depth, technical, liberal.

Collins, John J. *Daniel, 1–2 Maccabees, with Excursus on Apocalyptic Genre.* OTM. Wilmington, DE: Michael Glazier, 1984. One-to-several, semi-detailed, serious, liberal.

Goldingay, John E. *Daniel.* WBC. Dallas: Word Books, 1989. One-to-one, in-depth, technical, liberal.

Hammer, R. *The Book of Daniel.* CBCNEB. Cambridge: Cambridge University Press, 1976. One-to-one, semi-detailed, serious, liberal.

Howie, C. G.: see Ezekiel.

Jeffery, Arthur. *Daniel: Introduction and Exegesis.* IB. Nashville: Abingdon, 1952. One-to-several, semi-detailed, technical, liberal.

Keil, C. F. *The Book of Daniel.* K-D. Repr. Grand Rapids: Eerdmans, 1988. One-to-one, in-depth, technical, evangelical.

Leupold, Herbert C. *Exposition of Daniel.* Grand Rapids: Baker, 1969. One-to-one, semi-detailed, serious, evangelical.

Montgomery, J. A. *A Critical and Exegetical Commentary on the Book of Daniel.* ICC. Edinburgh: T. & T. Clark, 1927. One-to-one, in-depth, technical, liberal.

Russell, D. S. *Daniel.* DSB. Philadelphia: Westminster, 1981. One-to-one, detailed, popular, liberal.

Slotki, Judah J. *Daniel, Ezra, and Nehemiah.* Soncino Books of the

Bible. London: Soncino Press, 1951. One-to-one, detailed, serious, liberal.

Towner, W. Sibley. *Daniel*. INT. Atlanta: John Knox, 1984. One-to-one, detailed, serious, liberal.

Wallace, Ronald S. *The Message of Daniel*. TBST. Downers Grove, IL: InterVarsity, 1979. One-to-one, semi-detailed, serious, evangelical.

Wood, Leon. *A Commentary on Daniel*. Grand Rapids: Zondervan, 1973. One-to-one, detailed, serious, evangelical.

————. *Daniel*. BSC. Grand Rapids: Zondervan, 1975. One-to-one, semi-detailed, popular, evangelical.

Young, E. J. *The Prophecy of Daniel*. Grand Rapids: Eerdmans, 1949. Repr. *Commentary on Daniel*. London: Banner of Truth, 1972. One-to-one, detailed, technical, evangelical.

Hosea

Anderson, F. I., and Freedman, D. N. *Hosea*. AB 24. Garden City: Doubleday, 1980. One-to-one, in-depth, technical, conservative-moderate.

Garland, D. David. *Hosea*. BSC. Grand Rapids: Zondervan, 1975. One-to-one, semi-detailed, popular, evangelical.

Harper, W. R. *A Critical and Exegetical Commentary on Amos and Hosea*. ICC. Edinburgh: T. & T. Clark; New York: Scribner's, 1905. One-to-one, in-depth, technical, liberal.

Keil, C. F. *The Twelve Minor Prophets*. Vol. 1. K-D. Repr. Grand Rapids: Eerdmans, 1988. One-to-one, in-depth, technical, evangelical.

Kidner, Derek. *Love to the Loveless. The Story and Message of Hosea*. TBST. Leicester, England; Downers Grove, IL: InterVarsity, 1982. One-to-one, semi-detailed, serious, evangelical.

Knight, G. A. F. *Hosea*. TBC. London: SCM, 1960. One-to-one, semi-detailed, serious, liberal.

Limburg, James. *Hosea-Micah*. INT. Louisville: Westminster/John Knox, 1987. One-to-one, detailed, serious, liberal.

Mauchline, John. *Hosea*. IB. Nashville: Abingdon, 1952. One-to-several, semi-detailed, technical, liberal.

Mays, James. *Hosea, A Commentary*. OTL. Louisville: Westminster/John Knox, 1969. One-to-one, in-depth, technical, liberal.

McKeating, Henry: see Amos.

Snaith, Norman: see Amos.

Stuart, Douglas. *Hosea-Jonah.* WBC. Waco, TX: Word Books, 1987. One-to-one, in-depth, technical, evangelical.

Vawter, Bruce: see Amos.

Ward, J. M. *Hosea: A Theological Commentary.* New York: Harper and Row, 1966. One-to-one, detailed, serious, liberal.

Wolff, Hans Walter. *Hosea.* HERM. Philadelphia: Fortress, 1974. One-to-one, in-depth, technical, liberal.

Wood, Leon. *Hosea.* EBC. Grand Rapids: Zondervan, 1985. One-to-several, detailed, serious, evangelical.

Joel

Allen, Leslie C. *The Books of Joel, Obadiah, Jonah, and Micah.* NICOT. Grand Rapids: Eerdmans, 1976. One-to-one, in-depth, technical, conservative-moderate.

Allen, Ronald *Joel.* BSC. Grand Rapids: Zondervan, 1988. One-to-one, semi-detailed, popular, evangelical.

Bewer, J. A. *A Critical and Exegetical Commentary on the Book of Joel.* ICC. Edinburgh: T. & T. Clark, 1911. One-to-one, in-depth, technical, liberal.

Hubbard, David. *Joel and Amos.* TOTC. Downers Grove, IL: Inter-Varsity, 1989. One-to-one, detailed, serious, evangelical.

Jones, D. R.: see Isaiah.

Keil, C. F.: see Hosea.

Kodell, Jerome: see Lamentations.

Limburg, James: see Hosea.

Myers, J. *Hosea, Joel, Amos, Obadiah, and Jonah.* LBC. Atlanta: John Knox, 1959. One-to-one, semi-detailed, popular, liberal.

Patterson, Richard. *Joel.* EBC. Grand Rapids: Zondervan, 1985. One-to-several, detailed, serious, evangelical.

Stuart, Douglas: see Hosea.

Thompson, John. *Joel: Introduction and Exegesis.* IB. Nashville: Abingdon, 1952. One-to-several, semi-detailed, technical, liberal.

Watts, John D. W. *The Books of Joel, Obadiah, Jonah, Nahum, Habakkuk, and Zephaniah.* CBCNEB. New York: Cambridge University, 1975. One-to-several, semi-detailed, serious, conservative-moderate.

Wolff, Hans Walter. *Joel and Amos.* HERM. Philadelphia: Fortress, 1977. One-to-one, in-depth, technical, liberal.

Smith, J. P.; Ward, W. H.; and Bewer, J. A.: see Micah.

Amos

Anderson, Francis, and Freedman, David Noel. *Amos*. AB. Garden City: Doubleday, 1989. One-to-one, in-depth, technical, conservative-moderate.

Cohen, G. *Amos*. Everyman's Bible Commentary. Chicago: Moody Press, 1971. One-to-one, semi-detailed, popular, evangelical.

Fosbroke, Hughell. *Amos: Introduction and Exegesis*. IB. Nashville: Abingdon, 1952. One-to-several, semi-detailed, technical, liberal.

Garland, D. David. *Amos*. BSC. Grand Rapids: Zondervan, 1973. One-to-one, semi-detailed, popular, evangelical.

Hammershaimb, E. *The Book of Amos: A Commentary*. Oxford: Basil Blackwell, 1970. One-to-one, detailed, serious, liberal.

Harper, W. R.: see Hosea.

Hubbard, David: see Joel.

Keil, C. F.: see Hosea.

Limburg, James: see Hosea.

Marsh, J. *Amos and Micah*. TBC. London: SCM, 1959. One-to-one, semi-detailed, serious, liberal.

Martin-Achard, R., and Re'emi, S. P. *Amos and Lamentations: God's People in Crisis*. ITL. Grand Rapids: Eerdmans, 1984. One-to-one, detailed, serious, conservative-moderate.

Mays, James. *Amos, A Commentary*. OTL. Louisville: Westminster/John Knox, 1969. One-to-one, in-depth, technical, liberal.

McComiskey, Thomas. *Amos*. EBC. Grand Rapids: Zondervan, 1985. One-to-several, detailed, serious, evangelical.

McKeating, Henry. *The Books of Amos, Hosea, and Micah*. CBCNEB. New York: Cambridge University, 1971. One-to-several, semi-detailed, serious, liberal.

Motyer, J. A. *The Day of the Lion*. Leicester, England; Downers Grove, IL: InterVarsity, 1974. One-to-one, semi-detailed, serious, evangelical.

————. *The Message of Amos*. TBST. Downers Grove, IL: InterVarsity, 1988. One-to-one, semi-detailed, serious, evangelical.

Myers, J. M. *The Book of Jonah*. Richmond: John Knox, 1959. One-to-one, detailed, serious, liberal.

Smith, Gary. *Amos: A Commentary*. Grand Rapids: Zondervan, 1989. One-to-one, in-depth, technical, evangelical.

Snaith, Norman. *Amos, Hosea, and Micah*. London: Epworth Press, 1956. One-to-one, semi-detailed, serious, evangelical.

Stuart, Douglas: see Hosea.
Vawter, Bruce, CM. *Amos, Hosea, Micah, with Introduction to Classical Prophecy.* OTM. Wilmington, DE: Michael Glazier, 1981. One-to-one, semi-detailed, serious, liberal.
Wolff, Hans Walter: see Joel.

Obadiah

Allen, Leslie C.: see Joel.
Armerding, Carl. *Obadiah.* EBC. Grand Rapids: Zondervan, 1985. One-to-several, detailed, serious, evangelical.
Baker, David; Alexander, Desmond; and Waltke, Bruce. *Obadiah, Jonah, Micah.* TOTC. Downers Grove, IL: InterVarsity, 1989. One-to-one, detailed, serious, evangelical.
Coggins, R. J., and Re'emi, S. P.: see Nahum.
Eaton, J. H. *Obadiah, Nahum, Habakkuk, and Zephaniah.* TBC. London: SCM, 1961. One-to-several, semi-detailed, serious, liberal.
Keil, C. F.: see Hosea.
Kodell, Jerome: see Lamentations.
Limburg, James: see Hosea.
Myers, J.: see Joel.
Smith, J. P.; Ward, W. H.; and Bewer, J. A.: see Micah.
Stuart, Douglas: see Hosea.
Thompson, John. *Obadiah: Introduction and Exegesis.* IB. Nashville: Abingdon, 1957. One-to-several, semi-detailed, technical, liberal.
Walton, John and Beyer, Bryan. *Obadiah and Jonah.* BSC. Grand Rapids: Zondervan, 1988. One-to-one, semi-detailed, popular, evangelical.
Watts, John D. W. *Obadiah.* Grand Rapids: Eerdmans, 1969. One-to-one, in-depth, technical, conservative-moderate.
————. (CBCNEB): see Joel.
Wolff, Hans Walter. *Obadiah and Jonah.* CC. Minneapolis: Augsburg, 1986. One-to-one, in-depth, technical, liberal.

Jonah

Allen, Leslie C.: see Joel.
Baker, David, et al.: see Obadiah.
Banks, W. L. *Jonah: The Reluctant Prophet.* Everyman's Bible Commentary Series. Chicago: Moody Press, 1966. One-to-one, semi-detailed, popular, evangelical.

Craghan, John: see Esther.
Ellison, H. L. *Jonah.* EBC. Grand Rapids: Zondervan, 1985. One-to-several, detailed, serious, evangelical.
Fretheim, T. E. *The Message of Jonah: A Theological Commentary.* Minneapolis: Augsburg, 1977. One-to-one, detailed, serious, liberal.
Keil, C. F.: see Hosea.
Knight, G. A. F.: see Ruth.
Limburg, James: see Hosea.
Mitchell, H. J.; Smith, J. M. P.; and Bewer, J. A.: see Haggai.
Myers, J.: see Joel.
Smart, James. *Jonah: Introduction and Exegesis.* IB. Nashville: Abingdon, 1952. One-to-several, semi-detailed, technical, liberal.
Stuart, Douglas: see Hosea.
Walton, John; and Beyer, Bryan: see Obadiah.
Watts, John D. W.: see Joel.
Wolff, Hans Walter: see Obadiah.

Micah

Allen, Leslie C.: see Joel.
Baker, David, et al.: see Obadiah.
Hillers, Delbert. *Micah.* HERM. Philadelphia: Fortress, 1983. One-to-one, in-depth, technical, liberal.
Keil, C. F.: see Hosea.
Limburg, James: see Hosea.
Marsh, J.: see Amos.
Mays, James. *Micah, A Commentary.* OTL. Philadelphia: Westminster, 1976. One-to-one, in-depth, technical, liberal.
McComiskey, Thomas. *Micah.* EBC. Grand Rapids: Zondervan, 1985. One-to-several, detailed, serious, evangelical.
McKeating, Henry: see Amos.
Riggs, Jack. *Micah.* BSC. Grand Rapids: Zondervan, 1987. One-to-one, semi-detailed, popular, evangelical.
Smith, J. P.; Ward, W. H.; and Bewer, J. A. *A Critical and Exegetical Commentary on Micah, Zephaniah, Nahum, Habakkuk, Obadiah, and Joel.* ICC. New York: Scribner's, 1911. One-to-one, in-depth, technical, liberal.
Smith, Ralph L. *Micah-Malachi.* WBC. Waco, TX: Word Books, 1984. One-to-one, detailed, technical, evangelical.
Snaith, Norman: see Amos.
Vawter, Bruce: see Amos.

Wolfe, Rolland. *The Book of Micah: Introduction and Exegesis.* IB. Nashville: Abingdon, 1952. One-to-several, semi-detailed, technical, liberal.

Wolff, Hans Walter. *Micah.* CC. Minneapolis: Augsburg Fortress, 1990. One-to-one, in-depth, technical, liberal.

Nahum

Achtemeier, Elizabeth. *Nahum-Malachi.* INT. Atlanta: John Knox, 1986. One-to-one, detailed, serious, liberal.

Armerding, Carl. *Nahum.* EBC. Grand Rapids: Zondervan, 1985. One-to-several, detailed, serious, evangelical.

Baker, David. *Nahum, Habakkuk, Zephaniah.* TOTC. Downers Grove, IL: InterVarsity, 1988. One-to-one, semi-detailed, serious, evangelical.

Coggins, R. J. and Re'emi, S. P. *Nahum, Obadiah, Esther.* ITC. Grand Rapids: Eerdmans, 1985. One-to-several, semi-detailed, serious, liberal.

Eaton, J. H.: see Obadiah.

Heflin, J. N. Boo. *Nahum, Habakkuk, Zephaniah, and Haggai.* BSC. Grand Rapids: Zondervan, 1985. One-to-one, semi-detailed, popular, evangelical.

Keil, C. F. *The Twelve Minor Prophets.* Vol. 2. K-D. Repr. Grand Rapids: Eerdmans, 1988. One-to-one, in-depth, technical, evangelical.

Maier, Walter. *The Book of Nahum.* St. Louis: Concordia Publishing House, 1959. Repr. Grand Rapids: Baker Book House, 1980. One-to-one, in-depth, technical, evangelical.

Robertson, O. Palmer. *The Books of Nahum, Habakkuk, and Zephaniah.* NICOT. Grand Rapids: Eerdmans, 1989. One-to-one, detailed, serious, evangelical.

Smith, J. P.; Ward, W. H.; and Bewer, J. A.: see Micah.

Taylor, Charles, Jr. *The Book of Nahum: Introduction and Exegesis.* IB. Nashville: Abingdon, 1952. One-to-several, semi-detailed, technical, liberal.

Watts, John D. W.: see Joel.

Habakkuk

Achtemeier, Elizabeth: see Nahum.

Armerding, Carl. *Habakkuk.* EBC. Grand Rapids: Zondervan, 1985. One-to-several, detailed, serious, evangelical.

Baker, David: see Nahum.

Eaton, J. H.: see Obadiah.
Heflin, J. N. B.: see Nahum.
Keil, C. F.: see Nahum.
Robertson, O. Palmer: see Nahum.
Smith, J. P.; Ward, W. H.; and Bewer, J. A.: see Micah.
Taylor, Charles, Jr. *Habakkuk.* IB. Nashville: Abingdon, 1952. One-
   to-several, semi-detailed, technical, liberal.
Watts, John D. W.: see Joel.

Zephaniah

Achtemeier, Elizabeth: see Nahum.
Baker, David: see Nahum.
Eaton, J. H.: see Obadiah.
Heflin, J. N. B.: see Nahum.
Keil, C. F.: see Nahum.
Robertson, O. Palmer: see Nahum.
Smith, J. P.; Ward, W. H.; and Bewer, J. A.: see Micah.
Taylor, Charles, Jr. *The Book of Zephaniah: Introduction and Exegesis.*
   IB. Nashville: Abingdon, 1952. One-to-several, semi-detailed,
   technical, liberal.
Walker, Larry. *Zephaniah.* EBC. Grand Rapids: Zondervan, 1985.
   One-to-several, detailed, serious, evangelical.
Watts, John D. W.: see Joel.

Haggai

Achtemeier, Elizabeth: see Nahum.
Alden, Robert. *Haggai.* EBC. Grand Rapids: Zondervan, 1985.
   One-to-several, detailed, serious, evangelical.
Baldwin, Joyce. *Haggai, Zechariah, Malachi.* TOTC. Downers
   Grove, IL: InterVarsity, 1972. One-to-one, detailed, serious,
   evangelical.
Heflin, J. N. B.: see Nahum.
Keil, C. F.: see Nahum.
Kodell, Jerome: see Lamentations.
Mitchell, H. J.; Smith, J. M. P.; and Bewer, J. A. *Haggai, Zechariah,
   Malachi, and Jonah.* ICC. Edinburgh: T. & T. Clark, 1912. One-
   to-one, in-depth, technical, liberal.
Petersen, David. *Haggai and Zechariah 1–8, A Commentary.* OTL.
   Philadelphia: Westminster, 1984. One-to-one, in-depth, techni-
   cal, liberal.
Thomas, D. Winton. *The Book of Haggai: Introduction and Exegesis.*

IB. Nashville: Abingdon, 1952. One-to-several, semi-detailed, technical, liberal.

Verhoef, Pieter A. *The Books of Haggai and Malachi.* NICOT. Grand Rapids: Eerdmans, 1987. One-to one, in-depth, technical, evangelical.

Wolf, Herbert. *Haggai and Malachi: Rededication and Renewal.* Chicago: Moody Press, 1976. One-to-one, detailed, serious, evangelical.

Wolff, Hans Walter. *Haggai.* CC. Minneapolis: Augsburg, 1988. One-to-one, in-depth, technical, liberal.

Zechariah

Achtemeier, Elizabeth: see Nahum.

Baldwin, Joyce: see Haggai.

Barker, Kenneth. *Zechariah.* EBC. Grand Rapids: Zondervan, 1985. One-to-several, detailed, serious, evangelical.

Dentan, Robert. *Zechariah 9–14: Introduction and Exegesis.* IB. Nashville: Abingdon, 1952. One-to-several, semi-detailed, technical, liberal.

Heater, Homer, Jr. *Zechariah.* BSC. Grand Rapids: Zondervan, 1988. One-to-one, semi-detailed, popular, evangelical.

Keil, C. F.: see Nahum.

Kodell, Jerome: see Lamentations.

Mitchell, H. J.; Smith, J. M. P.; and Bewer, J. A.: see Haggai.

Thomas, D. Winton. *Zechariah 1–8: Introduction and Exegesis.* IB. Nashville: Abingdon, 1952. One-to-several, semi-detailed, technical, liberal.

Malachi

Achtemeier, Elizabeth: see Nahum.

Alden, Robert. *Malachi.* EBC. Grand Rapids: Zondervan, 1985. One-to-several, detailed, serious, evangelical.

Baldwin, Joyce: see Haggai.

Dentan, Robert. *The Book of Malachi: Introduction and Exegesis.* IB. Nashville: Abingdon, 1952. One-to-several, semi-detailed, technical, liberal.

Isbell, Charles. *Malachi.* BSC. Grand Rapids: Zondervan, 1980. One-to-one, semi-detailed, popular, evangelical.

Kaiser, Walter C., Jr. *Malachi: God's Unchanging Love.* Grand Rapids: Baker, 1984. One-to-one, in-depth, technical, evangelical.

Keil, C. F.: see Nahum.
Kodell, Jerome: see Lamentations.
Mitchell, H. J.; Smith, J. M. P.; and Bewer, J. A.: see Haggai.
Smith, J. M. P. *A Critical and Exegetical Commentary on the Book of Malachi.* Edinburgh: T. & T. Clark, 1912. One-to-one, in-depth, technical, liberal.
Verhoef, Pieter A.: see Haggai.
Wolf, Herbert: see Haggai.

NEW TESTAMENT

Matthew

Allen, W. C. *A Critical and Exegetical Commentary on St. Matthew.* 3d ed. ICC. Edinburgh: T. & T. Clark, 1922. One-to-one, in-depth, technical, liberal.
Argyle, A. W. *The Gospel according to Matthew.* CBCNEB. New York: Cambridge University, 1963. One-to-one, semi-detailed, serious, liberal.
Beare, Francis W. *The Gospel according to Matthew.* New York: Harper and Row, 1981. One-to-one, in-depth, technical, liberal.
Bruner, F. D. *Matthew, A Commentary.* Vol. 1 (Matt. 1–12) *The Christbook.* Dallas: Word Books, 1988. One-to-one, in-depth, serious, conservative-moderate.
————. *Matthew, A commentary.* Vol. 2 (Matt. 13–28) *The Churchbook.* Dallas: Word Books, 1990. One-to-one, in-depth, serious, conservative-moderate.
Carson, Donald. *Matthew.* EBC. Grand Rapids: Zondervan, 1984. One-to-one, in-depth, technical, evangelical.
————. *The Sermon on the Mount: An Evangelical Exposition of Matthew 5–7.* Grand Rapids: Baker, 1977. One-to-one, in-depth, technical, evangelical.
Carson, Donald. *When Jesus Confronts the World: An Evangelical Exposition of Matthew 8–10.* Grand Rapids: Baker, 1987. One-to-one, in-depth, technical, evangelical.
Davies, W. D., and Allison, Dale. *Matthew.* Vol. 1 (chs. 1–7); series replacement vol. for Allen, *St. Matthew*). ICC. Minneapolis: Augsburg Fortress, 1988. One-to-one, in-depth, technical, liberal.
Fenton, J. *St. Matthew.* 2d ed. Westminster Pelican Commentaries. Philadelphia: Westminster, 1977. One-to-one, detailed, serious, liberal.

France, Richard T. *Matthew*. TNTC. Grand Rapids: Eerdmans, 1987. One-to-one, detailed, serious, evangelical.

———. *Matthew: Evangelist and Teacher*. Grand Rapids: Zondervan, 1989. One-to-one, detailed, serious, evangelical.

Green, H. Benedict. *The Gospel according to Matthew in the Revised Standard Version*. New York: Oxford, 1975. One-to-one, semi-detailed, serious, liberal.

Guelich, Robert. *The Sermon on the Mount*. Waco, TX: Word Books, 1982. One-to-one, in-depth, technical, evangelical.

Gundry, Robert. *Matthew: A Commentary on His Literary and Theological Art*. Grand Rapids: Eerdmans, 1982. One-to-one, in-depth, technical, liberal.

Hendriksen, William. *The Gospel of Matthew*. Grand Rapids: Baker, 1976. One-to-one, detailed, serious, evangelical.

Hill, David. *The Gospel of Matthew*. Rev. ed. NCBC. Grand Rapids: Eerdmans, 1981. One-to-one, detailed, serious, liberal.

Johnson, Sherman. *Matthew*. IB. Nashville: Abingdon, 1952. One-to-several, semi-detailed, technical, liberal.

Kilgallan, John. *A Brief Commentary on the Gospel of Matthew*. Mahwah, NJ: Paulist Press, 1990. One-to-one, semi-detailed, serious, liberal.

Luz, Ulrich. *Matthew 1–7*. CC. Minneapolis: Augsburg Fortress, 1989. One-to-one, in-depth, technical, liberal.

Mann, C. S., and Albright, W. F. *Matthew*. AB. Garden City: Doubleday, 1971. One-to-one, semi-detailed, technical, conservative-moderate.

Meier, John P. *Matthew*. NTM. Wilmington, DE: Michael Glazier, 1979. One-to-one, semi-detailed, serious, liberal.

Schweizer, Eduard. *The Good News according to Matthew*. Atlanta: John Knox, 1974. One-to-one, in-depth, technical, liberal.

Smith, Robert. *Matthew*. ACNT. Minneapolis: Augsburg, 1988. One-to-one, detailed, serious, liberal.

Stott, John R. W. *The Message of the Sermon on the Mount*. TBST. Leicester, England; Downers Grove, IL: InterVarsity, 1988. One-to-one, semi-detailed, serious, evangelical.

Vos, Howard. *Matthew*. BSC. Grand Rapids: Zondervan, 1979. One-to-one, semi-detailed, popular, evangelical.

Mark

Anderson, Hugh. *The Gospel of Mark*. NCBC. Grand Rapids: Eerdmans, 1981. One-to-one, semi-detailed, technical, liberal.

Cole, R. Alan. *The Gospel according to St. Mark.* TNTC. Grand Rapids: Eerdmans, 1962. One-to-one, detailed, serious, evangelical.

Cranfield, C. E. B. *The Gospel according to Saint Mark.* Cambridge: Cambridge University Press, 1963. One-to-one, in-depth, technical, conservative-moderate.

Gould, E. P. *A Critical and Exegetical Commentary on the Gospel According to St. Mark.* ICC. Edinburgh: T. & T. Clark, 1907. One-to-one, in-depth, technical, liberal.

Grant, Frederick. *Mark.* IB. Nashville: Abingdon, 1952. One-to-several, semi-detailed, technical, liberal.

Guelich, Robert A. *Mark 1–8:26.* WBC. Waco, TX: Word Books, 1989. One-to-one, in-depth, technical, conservative-moderate.

Harrington, Wilfred, OP. *Mark.* NTM. Wilmington, DE: Michael Glazier, 1979. One-to-one, semi-detailed, serious, liberal.

Hendriksen, William. *The Gospel of Mark.* Grand Rapids: Baker, 1975. One-to-one, in-depth, serious, evangelical.

Hurtado, Larry. *Mark.* Good News Commentaries. San Francisco: Harper and Row, 1983. One-to-one, detailed, serious, conservative-moderate.

Johnson, Sherman. *A Commentary on the Gospel according to St. Mark.* HNTC. 2d ed. New York: Harper and Row, 1987. One-to-one, detailed, serious, liberal.

Kilgallan, John. *A Brief Commentary on the Gospel of Mark.* Mahwah, NJ: Paulist Press, 1989. One-to-one, semi-detailed, serious, liberal.

Lane, William L. *The Gospel of Mark.* NICNT. Grand Rapids: Eerdmans, 1973. One-to-one, in-depth, technical, evangelical.

Mann, C. S. *Mark.* AB. Garden City: Doubleday, 1986. One-to-one, detailed, technical, liberal.

Martin, Ralph. *Mark: Evangelist and Theologian.* Grand Rapids: Zondervan, 1973. One-to-one, semi-detailed, serious, evangelical.

Moule, C. F. D. *The Gospel according to Mark.* CBCNEB. New York: Cambridge University, 1965. One-to-one, semi-detailed, serious, liberal.

Nineham, Dennis. *The Gospel of St. Mark.* New York: Penguin Books, 1963. One-to-one, detailed, serious, liberal.

Schweizer, Eduard. *The Good News according to Mark.* Atlanta: John Knox, 1970. One-to-one, in-depth, technical, liberal.

Stock, Augustine, OSB. *The Method and Message of Mark.* Wilmington, DE: Michael Glazier, 1988. One-to-one, detailed, technical, liberal.

Taylor, Vincent. *The Gospel according to St. Mark.* 2d ed. New York: Macmillan, 1966; repr. Grand Rapids: Baker, 1981. One-to-one, detailed, serious, conservative-moderate.

Vos, Howard. *Mark.* BSC. Grand Rapids: Zondervan, 1979. One-to-one, semi-detailed, popular, evangelical.

Wessel, Walter. *Mark.* EBC. Grand Rapids: Zondervan, 1984. One-to-several, detailed, serious, evangelical.

Williamson, Lamar, Jr. *Mark.* INT. Atlanta: John Knox, 1983. One-to-one, detailed, serious, liberal.

Luke

Browning, Wilfred R. F. *Luke.* TBC. New York: Collier Books, 1962. One-to-one, semi-detailed, serious, liberal.

Caird, G. B. *The Gospel of St. Luke.* New York: Penguin, 1964. One-to-one, detailed, serious, liberal.

Danker, Frederick W. *Jesus and the New Age: A Commentary on St. Luke's Gospel.* Philadelphia: Fortress Press, 1988. One-to-one, detailed, serious, conservative-moderate.

Ellis, E. Earle. *The Gospel of Luke.* 2d ed. NCBC. Grand Rapids: Eerdmans, 1974. One-to-one, semi-detailed, technical, conservative-moderate.

Evans, C. F. *Saint Luke.* NTC. Philadelphia: Trinity, 1990. One-to-one, in-depth, technical, liberal.

Fitzmyer, Joseph. *The Gospel according to Luke.* 2 vols. AB. Garden City: Doubleday, 1981, 1985. One-to-one, in-depth, technical, liberal.

Geldenhuys, Norval. *The Gospel of Luke.* NICNT. Eerdmans, 1950. One-to-one, in-depth, serious, evangelical.

Gideon, Virtus. *Luke.* BSC. Grand Rapids: Zondervan, 1967. One-to-one, semi-detailed, popular, evangelical.

Gilmour, S. MacLean. *Luke.* IB. Nashville: Abingdon, 1952. One-to-several, semi-detailed, technical, liberal.

Godet, F. L. *Commentary on the Gospel of St. Luke.* 2 vols. Edinburgh: T. & T. Clark, 1870. One-to-one, in-depth, technical, liberal.

Hendriksen, William. *The Gospel of Luke.* Grand Rapids: Baker, 1978. One-to-several, detailed, serious, evangelical.

Kilgallan, John. *A Brief Commentary on the Gospel of Luke.* Mahwah, NJ: Paulist Press, 1988. One-to-one, semi-detailed, serious, liberal.

LaVerdiere, Eugene, SSS. *Luke.* NTM. Wilmington, DE: Michael Glazier, 1980. One-to-one, semi-detailed, serious, liberal.

Leaney, A. R. C. *A Commentary on the Gospel according to St. Luke.* HNTC. New York: Harper and Row, 1958. One-to-one, detailed, serious, liberal.

Liefeld, Walter. *Luke.* EBC. Grand Rapids: Zondervan, 1984. One-to-several, detailed, serious, evangelical.

Marshall, I. Howard. *The Gospel of Luke: A Commentary on the Greek Text.* NIGTC. Grand Rapids: Eerdmans, 1978. One-to-one, in-depth, technical, evangelical.

Morris, Leon. *Luke.* Rev. ed. TNTC. Grand Rapids: Eerdmans, 1983. One-to-one, semi-detailed, serious, evangelical.

Nolland, John. *Luke 1–9:20.* WBC. Dallas, TX: Word Books, 1989. One-to-one, in-depth, technical, evangelical.

Plummer, A. *A Critical and Exegetical Commentary on St. Luke.* 5th ed. ICC. Edinburgh: T. & T. Clark, 1901. One-to-one, in-depth, technical, liberal.

Schweizer, Eduard. *The Good News according to Luke.* Atlanta: John Knox, 1979. One-to-one, in-depth, technical, liberal.

Thompson, G. H. P. *The Gospel according to Luke.* New Clarendon Commentary on the New English Bible. Oxford: University Press, 1972. One-to-one, semi-detailed, serious, conservative-moderate.

Tiede, David L. *Luke.* ACNT. Minneapolis: Augsburg, 1988. One-to-one, detailed, serious, liberal.

Tinsley, E. J. *The Gospel according to Luke.* CBCNEB. New York: Cambridge University, 1965. One-to-one, semi-detailed, serious, liberal.

Wilcock, Michael. *The Message of Luke.* TBST. Leicester, England; Downers Grove, IL: InterVarsity, 1979. One-to-one, semi-detailed, serious, evangelical.

John

Barrett, C. K. *The Gospel according to St. John.* 2d ed. Philadelphia: Westminster, 1978. One-to-one, in-depth, technical, liberal.

Beasley-Murray, G. R. *John.* WBC. Waco, TX: Word Books, 1987. One-to-one, in-depth, technical, evangelical.

Bernard, J. H. *A Critical and Exegetical Commentary on the Gospel according to St. John.* 2 vols. ICC. Edinburgh: T. & T. Clark, 1928. One-to-one, in-depth, technical, liberal.

Brown, Raymond E. *The Gospel according to John.* 2 vols. AB. Garden City: Doubleday, 1966, 1970. One-to-one, in-depth, technical, liberal.

Bruce, F. F. *The Gospel of John.* Grand Rapids: Eerdmans, 1984. One-to-one, detailed, popular, evangelical.

Bultmann, Rudolph. *The Gospel of John: A Commentary.* Philadelphia: Westminster, 1971. One-to-one, in-depth, technical, liberal.

Carson, D. A. *The Farewell Discourse and Final Prayer of Jesus: An Evangelical Exposition of John 14–17.* Grand Rapids: Baker, 1981. One-to-one, in-depth, technical, evangelical.

Haenchen, Ernst. *Gospel of John.* 2 vols. HERM. Philadelphia: Fortress, 1984. One-to-one, in-depth, technical, liberal.

Hendriksen, William. *The Gospel of John.* Grand Rapids: Baker, 1961. One-to-one, detailed, serious, evangelical.

Hobbs, Herschel. *John.* BSC. Grand Rapids: Zondervan, 1973. One-to-one, summary, popular, evangelical.

Howard, Wilbert. *John.* IB. Nashville: Abingdon, 1952. One-to-several, semi-detailed, technical, liberal.

Hunter, Archibald M. *The Gospel according to John.* CBCNEB. New York: Cambridge University, 1965. One-to-one, semi-detailed, serious, liberal.

Kysar, Robert. *John.* ACNT. Minneapolis: Augsburg, 1985. One-to-one, detailed, serious, conservative-moderate.

Lindars, Barnabas. *John.* NCBC. Grand Rapids: Eerdmans, 1981. One-to-one, semi-detailed, technical, liberal.

McPolin, James, SJ. *John.* NTM. Wilmington, DE: Michael Glazier, 1979. One-to-one, semi-detailed, serious, liberal.

Morris, Leon. *The Gospel of John.* NICNT. Grand Rapids: Eerdmans, 1970. One-to-one, in-depth, technical, evangelical.

———. *Reflections on the Gospel of John, Vol. 1.* [John 1–5]. Grand Rapids: Baker, 1986. One-to-one, detailed, serious, evangelical.

Morris, Leon. *Reflections on the Gospel of John, Vol. 2.* [John 6–10]. Grand Rapids: Baker, 1987. One-to-one, detailed, serious, evangelical.

Morris, Leon. *Reflections on the Gospel of John, Vol. 3.* [John 11–16]. Grand Rapids: Baker, 1988. One-to-one, detailed, serious, evangelical.

Morris, Leon. *Reflections on the Gospel of John, Vol. 4.* [John 17-21]. Grand Rapids: Baker, 1989. One-to-one, detailed, serious, evangelical.

Schnackenburg, Rudolph. *The Gospel according to St. John.* 3 vols. New York: Crossroad/Continuum, 1980, 1982. One-to-one, in-depth, technical, liberal.

Sloyan, Gerard. *John.* INT. Atlanta: John Knox, 1987. One-to-one, detailed, serious, liberal.

Tasker, R. V. G. *John.* TNTC. Grand Rapids: Eerdmans, 1969. One-to-one, semi-detailed, serious, evangelical.

Tenney, Merrill. *John.* EBC. Grand Rapids: Zondervan, 1981. One-to-several, semi-detailed, popular, evangelical.

Acts

Bruce, F. F. *The Acts of the Apostles.* 3d ed., revised and enlarged. Grand Rapids: Eerdmans, 1989. One-to-one, in-depth, technical, evangelical.

————. *The Book of Acts.* Revised edition. NICNT. Grand Rapids: Eerdmans, 1954. One-to-one, detailed, technical, evangelical.

Conzelmann, Hans. *Acts.* HERM. Philadelphia: Fortress, 1987. One-to-one, in-depth, technical, liberal.

Crowe, Jerome, CP. *The Acts.* NTM. Wilmington, DE: Michael Glazier, 1980. One-to-one, semi-detailed, serious, liberal.

Haenchen, Ernst. *The Acts of the Apostles, A Commentary.* Philadelphia: Westminster, 1971. One-to-one, in-depth, technical, liberal.

Harrison, Everett F. *Acts: The Expanding Church.* Chicago: Moody Press, 1975. One-to-one, detailed, serious, liberal.

Kilgallan, John. *A Brief Commentary on the Acts of the Apostles.* Mahwah, NJ: Paulist Press, 1988. One-to-one, semi-detailed, serious, liberal.

Kroder, Gerhard. *Acts.* ACNT. Minneapolis: Augsburg Fortress, 1986. One-to-one, detailed, serious, liberal.

Longenecker, Richard. *Acts.* EBC. Grand Rapids: Zondervan, 1981. One-to-several, detailed, serious, evangelical.

Macgregor, G. H. C. *Acts.* IB. Nashville: Abingdon, 1952. One-to-several, semi-detailed, technical, liberal.

Marshall, I. Howard. *Acts.* TNTC. Grand Rapids: Eerdmans, 1980. One-to-one, detailed, serious, evangelical.

Munck, Johannes. *Acts.* AB. Garden City: Doubleday, 1967. One-to-one, semi-detailed, technical, liberal.

Neil, William. *Acts.* NCBC. New ed. Grand Rapids: Eerdmans, 1983. One-to-one, semi-detailed, technical, liberal.

Vaughan, Curtis. *Acts.* BSC. Grand Rapids: Zondervan, 1974. One-to-one, semi-detailed, popular, evangelical.

Williams, C. S. C. *A Commentary on the Acts of the Apostles.* HNTC. New York: Harper and Row, 1987. One-to-one, detailed, serious, liberal.

Willimon, William. *Acts.* INT. Louisville: Westminster/John Knox, 1988. One-to-one, semi-detailed, serious, liberal.

Romans

Achtemeier, Paul. *Romans.* INT. Atlanta: John Knox, 1985. One-to-one, detailed, serious, liberal.

Barrett, C. K. *A Commentary on the Epistle to the Romans.* HNTC. New York: Harper and Row, 1957. One-to-one, detailed, serious, conservative-moderate.

Best, Ernest. *The Letter of Paul to the Romans.* CBCNEB. New York: Cambridge University, 1967. One-to-one, semi-detailed, serious, liberal.

Black, Matthew. *Romans.* 2d ed. NCBC. Grand Rapids: Eerdmans, 1989. One-to-one, semi-detailed, technical, liberal.

Bruce, F. F. *Romans.* Rev. ed. TNTC. Grand Rapids: Eerdmans, 1983. One-to-one, detailed, serious, evangelical.

Cranfield, C. E. B. *Romans.* 2 vols. [series replacement for Sanday and Headlam, *Romans*]. ICC. Edinburgh: T. & T. Clark, 1975, 1979. One-to-one, in-depth, technical, liberal.

Dunn, James D. G. *Romans 1–8.* WBC. Waco, TX: Word Books, 1988. One-to-one, in-depth, technical, conservative-moderate.

———. *Romans 9–16.* WBC. Waco, TX: Word Books, 1988. One-to-one, in-depth, technical, conservative-moderate.

———. *Commentary on Romans.* [Abbrev. of above.] Grand Rapids: Eerdmans, 1985. One-to-one, detailed, serious, liberal.

Harrison, Everett F. *Romans.* EBC. Grand Rapids: Zondervan, 1976. One-to-several, detailed, serious, evangelical.

Harrisville, Roy. *Romans.* Minneapolis: Augsburg, 1980. One-to-one, detailed, serious, liberal.

Hendriksen, William. *Romans.* 2 vols. Grand Rapids: Baker, 1980, 1981. One-to-one, detailed, serious, evangelical.

Hunter, Archibald M. *The Epistle to the Romans.* TBC. London: SCM, 1955. One-to-one, semi-detailed, serious, liberal.

Käsemann, Ernst. *Commentary on Romans.* Grand Rapids: Eerdmans, 1980. One-to-one, in-depth, technical, liberal.

Knox, John. *Romans.* IB. Nashville: Abingdon, 1952. One-to-several, semi-detailed, technical, liberal.

Maly, Eugene. *Romans.* NTM. Wilmington, DE: Michael Glazier, 1980. One-to-one, semi-detailed, serious, liberal.

Morris, Leon. *The Epistle to the Romans.* Downers Grove, IL: Inter-Varsity, 1988. One-to-one, detailed, serious, evangelical.

Murray, John. *The Book of Romans.* NICNT. Grand Rapids: Eerdmans, 1968. One-to-one, detailed, technical, evangelical.

Sanday, W., and Headlam, A. C. *A Critical and Exegetical Commentary on Paul's Epistle to the Romans.* 5th ed. ICC. Edinburgh: T. & T. Clark, 1902. One-to-one, in-depth, technical, liberal.

Stott, John R. W. *Men Made New: An Exposition of Romans 5–8.* Grand Rapids: Baker, 1984. One-to-one, detailed, serious, evangelical.

Vaughan, Curtis, and Corley, Bruce. *Romans.* BSC. Grand Rapids: Zondervan, 1976. One-to-one, semi-detailed, popular, evangelical.

Zeisler, John. *Paul's Letter to the Romans.* NTC. Philadelphia: Trinity, 1989. One-to-one, in-depth, technical, liberal.

1 Corinthians

Barclay, William. *The Letters to the Corinthians.* 2d ed. DSB. Philadelphia: Westminster, 1956. One-to-one, semi-detailed, popular, conservative-moderate.

Barrett, C. K. *A Commentary on the First Epistle to the Corinthians.* HNTC. New York: Harper and Row, 1968. One-to-one, detailed, serious, liberal.

Bruce, F. F. *1 and 2 Corinthians.* NCBC. Grand Rapids: Eerdmans, 1981. One-to-one, detailed, serious, evangelical.

Carson, D. A. *Showing the Spirit: A Theological Exposition of 1 Corinthians 12–14.* Grand Rapids: Baker, 1987. One-to-one, in-depth, technical, evangelical.

Conzelmann, Hans. *1 Corinthians.* HERM. Philadelphia: Fortress, 1975. One-to-one, in-depth, technical, liberal.

Craig, Clarence T. *1 Corinthians.* IB. Nashville: Abingdon, 1957. One-to-several, semi-detailed, technical, liberal.

Fee, Gordon D. *1 Corinthians.* NICNT. Grand Rapids: Eerdmans, 1987. One-to-one, in-depth, technical, evangelical.

Gromacki, R. G. *Called to Be Saints: An Exposition of I Corinthians.* Grand Rapids: Eerdmans, 1977. One-to-one, detailed, serious, evangelical.

Grosheide, F. W. *Commentary on the First Epistle to the Corinthians.*

NICNT. Grand Rapids: Eerdmans, 1953. One-to-one, detailed, serious, evangelical.

Harrisville, Roy. *I Corinthians*. ACNT. Minneapolis: Augsburg, 1987. One-to-one, detailed, serious, conservative-moderate.

Holladay, Carl. *The First Letter of Paul to the Corinthians*. Austin: Abilene Christian University, 1984. One-to-one, detailed, serious, liberal.

MacArthur, John F. *I Corinthians*. Chicago: Moody, 1984. One-to-one, detailed, popular, evangelical.

Mare, W. Harold. *1 Corinthians*. EBC. Grand Rapids: Zondervan, 1976. One-to-several, detailed, serious, evangelical.

Morris, Leon. *1 Corinthians*. Rev. ed. TNTC. Grand Rapids: Eerdmans, 1983. One-to-one, detailed, serious, evangelical.

Murphy-O'Connor, Jerome, OP. *1 Corinthians*. NTM. Wilmington, DE: Michael Glazier, 1979. One-to-one, semi-detailed, serious, liberal.

Prior, David. *The Message of 1 Corinthians*. TBST. Downers Grove, IL: InterVarsity, 1982. One-to-one, semi-detailed, serious, evangelical.

Robertson, A., and Plummer, A. *1 Corinthians*. 2d ed. ICC. Edinburgh: T. & T. Clark, 1914. One-to-one, in-depth, technical, liberal.

Ruef, J. S. *Paul's First Letter to Corinth*. Philadelphia: Westminster, 1978. One-to-one, detailed, serious, liberal.

Thrall, Margaret. *The First and Second Letters of Paul to the Corinthians*. CBCNEB. Cambridge: Cambridge University Press, 1965. One-to-one, semi-detailed, serious, liberal.

Vaughan, Curtis, and Lea, Thomas. *1 Corinthians*. BSC. Grand Rapids: Zondervan, 1983. One-to-one, semi-detailed, popular, evangelical.

Walther, J. A. *I Corinthians*. AB. Garden City: Doubleday, 1976. One-to-one, semi-detailed, technical, liberal.

2 Corinthians

Barnett, Paul. *The Message of 2 Corinthians*. TBST. Leicester, England; Downers Grove, IL: InterVarsity, 1989. One-to-one, semi-detailed, serious, evangelical.

Barrett, C. K. *A Commentary on the Second Epistle to the Corinthians*. HNTC. New York: Harper and Row, 1974. One-to-one, detailed, technical, conservative-moderate.

Best, Ernest. *Second Corinthians.* INT. Louisville: Westminster/ John Knox, 1987. One-to-one, detailed, serious, liberal.

Betz, Hans D. *Second Corinthians 8 and 9.* HERM. Philadelphia: Fortress, 1985. One-to-one, in-depth, technical, liberal.

Bruce, F. F.: see 1 Corinthians.

Carson, D. A. *From Triumphalism to Maturity: An Exposition of 2 Corinthians 10–13.* Grand Rapids: Baker, 1984. One-to-one, in-depth, technical, evangelical.

Danker, Frederick. *II Corinthians.* ACNT. Minneapolis: Augsburg Fortress, 1989. One-to-one, detailed, serious, conservative-moderate.

Fallon, Frank. *2 Corinthians.* NTM. Wilmington, DE: Michael Glazier, 1980. One-to-one, semi-detailed, serious, liberal.

Filson, Floyd. *The Second Epistle to the Corinthians.* IB. Nashville: Abingdon, 1952. One-to-several, semi-detailed, technical, liberal.

Furnish, Victor Paul. *II Corinthians.* AB. Garden City: Doubleday, 1984. One-to-one, in-depth, technical, liberal.

Hanson, R. P. C. *2 Corinthians.* TBC. London: SCM, 1967. One-to-one, semi-detailed, serious, liberal.

Harris, Murray. *2 Corinthians.* EBC. Grand Rapids: Zondervan, 1976. One-to-several, detailed, serious, evangelical.

Hughes, Philip E. *Paul's Second Epistle to the Corinthians.* NICNT. Grand Rapids: Eerdmans, 1962. One-to-one, in-depth, technical, evangelical.

Kruse, Colin. *2 Corinthians.* TNTC. Grand Rapids: Eerdmans, 1987. One-to-one, detailed, serious, evangelical.

Martin, Ralph P. *2 Corinthians.* WBC. Waco, TX: Word Books, 1985. One-to-one, in-depth, technical, conservative-moderate.

Plummer, A. *A Critical and Exegetical Commentary on the Second Epistle of Paul to the Corinthians.* ICC. Edinburgh: T. & T. Clark, 1915. One-to-one, in-depth, technical, liberal.

Spencer, Aida and William. *2 Corinthians.* BSC. Grand Rapids: Zondervan, 1989. One-to-one, semi-detailed, popular, evangelical.

Tasker, R. V. G. *2 Corinthians.* TNTC. Grand Rapids: Eerdmans, 1958. One-to-one, detailed, serious, evangelical.

Thrall, Margaret: see 1 Corinthians.

Galatians

Betz, Hans Dieter. *Galatians.* HERM. Philadelphia: Fortress, 1979. One-to-one, in-depth, technical, liberal.

Bligh, John. *Galatians*. London: St. Paul Publishers, 1969. One-to-one, detailed, serious, liberal.

Bruce, F. F. *Galatians*. NIGTC. Grand Rapids: Eerdmans, 1982. One-to-one, in-depth, technical, evangelical.

Burton, E. de W. *Galatians*. ICC. Edinburgh: T. & T. Clark, 1921. One-to-one, in-depth, technical, liberal.

Cole, R. Alan. *Galatians*. TNTC. Grand Rapids: Eerdmans, 1983. One-to-one, detailed, serious, evangelical.

Cousar, Charles. *Galatians*. INT. Atlanta: John Knox, 1982. One-to-one, detailed, serious, liberal.

Fung, Ronald Y. K. *The Epistle to the Galatians*. NICNT. Grand Rapids: Eerdmans, 1988. One-to-one, detailed, serious, evangelical.

Guthrie, Donald. *Galatians*. NCBC. New York: Thomas Nelson and Sons, 1969. One-to-one, semi-detailed, technical, evangelical.

Hendriksen, William. *Galatians and Ephesians*. Grand Rapids: Baker, 1981. One-to-several, semi-detailed, serious, evangelical.

Krentz, Edgar. *Galatians*. [Bound with Philippians, Philemon, I Thessalonians.] ACNT. Minneapolis: Augsburg, 1985. One-to-one, detailed, serious, conservative-moderate.

Neil, William. *The Letter of Paul to the Galatians*. CBCNEB. Cambridge: Cambridge University Press, 1967. One-to-one, semi-detailed, serious, liberal.

Osiek, Carolyn, RSCJ. *Galatians*. NTM. Wilmington, DE: Michael Glazier, 1980. One-to-one, summary, serious, liberal.

Ridderbos, H. N. *The Epistle of Paul to the Churches of Galatia*. NICNT. Grand Rapids: Eerdmans, 1953. One-to-one, detailed, serious, evangelical.

Stamm, Raymond. *Galatians*. IB. Nashville: Abingdon, 1952. One-to-several, semi-detailed, technical, liberal.

Stott, John R. W. *Only One Way: The Message of Galatians*. TBST. Leicester, England; Downers Grove, IL: InterVarsity, 1988. One-to-one, semi-detailed, serious, evangelical.

Vaughan, Curtis. *Galatians*. BSC. Grand Rapids: Zondervan, 1972. One-to-one, semi-detailed, popular, evangelical.

Ephesians

Abbott, E. D. *Ephesians and Colossians*. ICC. Edinburgh: T. & T. Clark, 1897. One-to-one, in-depth, technical, liberal.

Barth, Markus. *Ephesians.* 2 vols. AB. Garden City: Doubleday, 1975. One-to-one, in-depth, technical, liberal.

Beare, Francis W. *Ephesians.* IB. Nashville: Abingdon, 1952. One-to-several, semi-detailed, technical, liberal.

Bruce, F. F.: see Colossians.

Caird, George B. *Paul's Letters from Prison (Ephesians, Philippians, Colossians, Philemon) in the Revised Standard Version.* New York: Oxford, 1977. One-to several, semi-detailed, serious, liberal.

Foulkes, Francis. *Ephesians.* Rev. Ed. TNTC. Grand Rapids: Eerdmans, 1983. One-to-one, semi-detailed, serious, evangelical.

Hendriksen, William: see Galatians.

Houlden, J. Leslie: see Philippians.

Mitton, C. Leslie. *Ephesians.* NCBC. Grand Rapids: Eerdmans, 1982. One-to-one, detailed, technical, liberal.

Simpson, E. K. *Commentary on the Epistles to the Ephesians and Colossians.* NICNT. Grand Rapids: Eerdmans, 1958. One-to-one, in-depth, serious, evangelical.

Swain, Lionel. *Ephesians.* NTM. Wilmington, DE: Michael Glazier, 1980. One-to-one, semi-detailed, serious, liberal.

Stott, John R. W. *The Message of Ephesians.* TBST. Leicester, England; Downers Grove, IL: InterVarsity, 1988. One-to-one, semi-detailed, serious, evangelical.

Taylor, Walter, Jr. *Ephesians.* ACNT. Bound with Colossians. Minneapolis: Augsburg, 1985. One-to-one, detailed, serious, liberal.

Thompson, G. H. P. *The Letters of Paul to the Ephesians, Colossians, and Philemon.* CBCNEB. Cambridge: Cambridge University Press, 1967. One-to-several, semi-detailed, serious, liberal.

Vaughan, Curtis. *Ephesians.* BSC. Grand Rapids: Zondervan, 1977. One-to-one, semi-detailed, popular, evangelical.

Wood, A. Skevington. *Ephesians.* EBC. Grand Rapids: Zondervan, 1978. One-to-several, detailed, serious, evangelical.

Philippians

Beare, F. W. *A Commentary on the Epistle to the Philippians.* HNTC. New York: Harper and Row, 1959. One-to-one, detailed, serious, liberal.

Bruce, F. F. *Philippians.* GNC. San Francisco: Harper and Row, 1983. One-to-one, semi-detailed, serious, evangelical.

Caird, George B.: see Ephesians.

Craddock, Fred. *Philippians.* INT. Louisville: Westminster/John Knox, 1984. One-to-one, semi-detailed, serious, liberal.

Getty, Mary Ann. *Philippians and Philemon.* NTM. Wilmington, DE: Michael Glazier, 1980. One-to-one, semi-detailed, serious, liberal.

Grayston, K. *The Letters of Paul to the Galatians and to the Philippians.* Cambridge: Cambridge University Press, 1967. One-to-one, detailed, serious, liberal.

Hawthorne, Gerald. *Philippians.* WBC. Waco, TX: Word Books, 1983. One-to-one, in-depth, technical, evangelical.

Hendriksen, William. *Philippians, Colossians, and Philemon.* Grand Rapids: Baker, 1962. One-to-several, semi-detailed, serious, evangelical.

Houlden, J. Leslie. *Paul's Letters From Prison: Philippians, Colossians, Philemon & Ephesians.* London: SCM, 1977. Philadelphia: Westminster, 1978. One-to-several, semi-detailed, serious, liberal.

Kent, Homer, Jr. *Philippians.* EBC. Grand Rapids: Zondervan, 1978. One-to-several, semi-detailed, serious, evangelical.

Koenig, John. *Philippians, Philemon.* ACNT. Minneapolis: Augsburg, 1989. One-to-several, detailed, serious, conservative-moderate.

Martin, Ralph P. *The Epistle of Paul to the Philippians.* NCBC. Grand Rapids: Eerdmans, 1980. One-to-one, detailed, serious, conservative-moderate.

———. *Philippians.* Rev. ed. TNTC. Grand Rapids: Eerdmans, 1983. One-to-one, detailed, serious, conservative-moderate.

Motyer, J. A. *The Message of Philippians.* TBST. Leicester, England; Downers Grove, IL: InterVarsity, 1984. One-to-one, semi-detailed, serious, evangelical.

Moule, Handley C. G. *The Epistle to the Philippians.* Grand Rapids: Baker, 1981. One-to-one, detailed, technical, evangelical.

Müller, J. J. *The Epistles of Paul to the Philippians and to Philemon.* NICNT. Grand Rapids: Eerdmans, 1955. One-to-one, detailed, serious, evangelical.

Scott, Ernest F. *The Epistle to the Philippians.* IB. Nashville: Abingdon, 1952. One-to-several, semi-detailed, technical, liberal.

Vincent, M. R. *A Critical and Exegetical Commentary on the Epistles to the Philippians and to Philemon.* ICC. Edinburgh: T. & T. Clark, 1897. One-to-one, in-depth, technical, liberal.

Vos, Howard. *Philippians.* BSC. Grand Rapids: Zondervan, 1980. One-to-one, semi-detailed, popular, evangelical.

Colossians

Abbott, T. K.: see Ephesians.

Beare, Francis W. *The Epistle to the Colossians*. IB. Nashville: Abingdon, 1955. One-to-several, semi-detailed, technical, liberal.

Bruce, F. F. *The Epistles to the Colossians, to Philemon, and to the Ephesians*. Rev. ed. NICNT. Grand Rapids: Eerdmans, 1984. One-to-one, detailed, serious, evangelical.

Caird, George B.: see Ephesians.

Carson, H. M. *The Epistles of Paul to the Colossians and Philemon*. TNTC. Grand Rapids: Eerdmans, 1960. One-to-one, detailed, serious, evangelical.

Hendriksen, William: see Philippians.

Houlden, J. Leslie: see Philippians.

Lohse, E. *Colossians and Philemon*. HERM. Philadelphia: Fortress, 1971. One-to-one, in-depth, technical, liberal.

Lucas, R. C. *The Message of Colossians and Philemon*. TBST. Leicester, England; Downers Grove, IL: InterVarsity, 1988. One-to-one, semi-detailed, serious, evangelical.

Martin, Ralph P. *Colossians and Philemon*. 3d ed. NCBC. Grand Rapids: Eerdmans, 1981. One-to-one, semi-detailed, technical, conservative-moderate.

McDonald, H. Dermot. *Commentary on Colossians and Philemon*. Waco, TX: Word Books, 1980. One-to-one, detailed, popular, evangelical.

Moule, C. F. D. *The Epistles of Paul the Apostle to the Colossians and to Philemon*. CBCNEB. New York: Cambridge University, 1957. One-to-one, semi-detailed, serious, liberal.

O'Brien, Peter F. *Colossians, Philemon*. WBC. Waco, TX: Word Books, 1982. One-to-one, in-depth, technical, evangelical.

Reumann, John. *Colossians*. [Bound with Ephesians.] ACNT. Minneapolis: Augsburg, 1985. One-to-one, detailed, serious, liberal.

Rogers, Patrick V., CP. *Colossians*. NTM. Wilmington, DE: Michael Glazier, 1980. One-to-one, semi-detailed, serious, liberal.

Schweizer, Eduard. *The Letter to the Colossians*. Minneapolis: Augsburg, 1982. One-to-one, detailed, technical, liberal.

Vaughan, Curtis. *Colossians*. EBC. Grand Rapids: Zondervan, 1978. One-to-several, detailed, serious, evangelical.

———. *Colossians and Philemon*. BSC. Grand Rapids: Zondervan, 1981. One-to-one, semi-detailed, popular, evangelical.

Wright, N. T. *The Epistles of Paul to the Colossians and to Philemon.* TNTC. Grand Rapids: Eerdmans, 1988. One-to-one, detailed, serious, evangelical.

1 Thessalonians

Bailey, John W. *I and II Thessalonians.* IB. Nashville: Abingdon, 1952. One-to-several, semi-detailed, technical, liberal.

Best, Ernest. *A Commentary on the First and Second Epistles to the Thessalonians.* HNTC. New York: Harper and Row, 1972. One-to-one, in-depth, technical, conservative-moderate.

Bruce, F. F. *1 & 2 Thessalonians.* WBC. Waco, TX: Word Books, 1982. One-to-one, in-depth, technical, evangelical.

Findlay, G. G. *The Epistles of Paul the Apostle to the Thessalonians.* Repr. Grand Rapids: Baker, 1982. One-to-one, detailed, technical, evangelical.

Frame, J. E. *The Epistles of St. Paul to the Thessalonians.* ICC. Edinburgh: T. & T. Clark, 1912. One-to-one, in-depth, technical, liberal.

Grayston, K. *The Letters of Paul to the Philippians and to the Thessalonians.* CBCNEB. Cambridge: Cambridge University Press, 1967. One-to-one, semi-detailed, serious, liberal.

Hendriksen, William. *Thessalonians, First and Second.* Grand Rapids: Baker, 1953. One-to-one, detailed, serious, evangelical.

————. *Thessalonians, Timothy, and Titus.* Grand Rapids: Baker, 1983. [Includes above.] One-to-several, detailed, serious, evangelical.

Hubbard, D. A. *Thessalonians.* Waco, TX: Word Books, 1977. One-to-one, semi-detailed, serious, evangelical.

Juel, Donald. *I Thessalonians.* ACNT. Minneapolis: Augsburg Fortress, 1989. One-to-several, detailed, serious, liberal.

Lünemann, G. *A Critical and Exegetical Commentary on the Epistles to the Thessalonians.* ICC. Edinburgh: T. & T. Clark, l880. One-to-one, in-depth, technical, liberal.

Marshall, I. Howard. *1 and 2 Thessalonians.* NCBC. Grand Rapids: Eerdmans, 1983. One-to-one, detailed, technical, evangelical.

Moore, Arthur L. *I and II Thessalonians.* NCBC. London: Nelson, 1969. One-to-one, semi-detailed, serious, conservative-moderate.

Morris, Leon. *The First and Second Epistles to the Thessalonians.*

NICNT. Grand Rapids: Eerdmans, 1959. One-to-one, detailed, technical, evangelical.

——. *The Epistles of Paul to the Thessalonians.* New ed. TNTC. Grand Rapids: Eerdmans, 1983. One-to-one, semi-detailed, serious, evangelical.

Neil, William. *Thessalonians.* Naperville, IL: Allenson, 1950. One-to-one, semi-detailed, serious, conservative-moderate.

Palmer, Earl. *1 and 2 Thessalonians.* GNC. New York: Harper and Row,1983. One-to-one, semi-detailed, popular, evangelical.

Reese, James M. *1 and 2 Thessalonians.* NTM. Wilmington, DE: Michael Glazier, 1979. One-to-one, semi-detailed, serious, liberal.

Thomas, Robert. *1 and 2 Thessalonians.* EBC. Grand Rapids: Zondervan, 1978. One-to-several, detailed, serious, evangelical.

Walvoord, John. *The Thessalonian Epistles.* BSC. Grand Rapids: Zondervan, 1967. One-to-one, semi-detailed, popular, evangelical.

Ward, Ronald A. *Commentary on 1 & 2 Thessalonians.* Waco, TX: Word Books, 1973. One-to-one, detailed, popular, evangelical.

2 Thessalonians

Aus, Roger. *II Thessalonians.* ACNT. Minneapolis: Augsburg, 1984. One-to-several, detailed, serious, conservative-moderate.

Bailey, John: see 1 Thessalonians.

Best, Ernest: see 1 Thessalonians.

Bruce, F. F.: see 1 Thessalonians.

Findlay, G. G.: see 1 Thessalonians.

Frame, J. E.: see 1 Thessalonians.

Grayston, K.: see 1 Thessalonians.

Hendriksen, William: see 1 Thessalonians.

Hubbard, D. A.: see 1 Thessalonians.

Marshall, I. Howard: see 1 Thessalonians.

Moore, Arthur L.: see 1 Thessalonians.

Morris, Leon (NICNT): see 1 Thessalonians.

—— (TNTC): see 1 Thessalonians.

Palmer, Earl: see 1 Thessalonians.

Reese, James: see 1 Thessalonians.

Thomas, Robert: see 1 Thessalonians.

Walvoord, John: see 1 Thessalonians.

Ward, Ronald A.: see 1 Thessalonians.

1 Timothy

Barclay, W. *The Letters to Timothy, Titus, and Philemon.* Rev. ed. DSB. Philadelphia: Westminster, 1975. One-to-one, semi-detailed, popular, conservative-moderate.

Barrett, C. K. *The Pastoral Epistles.* Oxford: Clarendon Press, 1963. One-to-one, detailed, serious, conservative-moderate.

Bernard, J. H. *The Pastoral Epistles.* repr. Grand Rapids: Baker, 1980. One-to-several, semi-detailed, technical, evangelical.

Blaiklock, E. M. *The Pastoral Epistles.* BSC. Grand Rapids: Zondervan, 1972. One-to-one, semi-detailed, popular, evangelical.

Dibelius, Martin, and Conzelmann, Hans. *The Pastoral Epistles.* HERM. Philadelphia: Fortress, 1972. One-to-one, in-depth, technical, liberal.

Earle, Ralph. *1 Timothy.* EBC. Grand Rapids: Zondervan, 1978. One-to-several, detailed, serious, evangelical.

Fee, Gordon. *1 and 2 Timothy, Titus.* GNC. San Francisco: Harper and Row, 1984. One-to-one, in-depth, serious, evangelical.

———. *1 and 2 Timothy, Titus.* NIBC [repr. of above based on NIV rather than **GNB**]. Peabody, MA: Hendrickson, 1988. One-to-one, in-depth, serious, evangelical.

Gealy, Fred D. *The First and Second Epistles to Timothy and the Epistle to Titus.* IB. Nashville: Abingdon, 1955. One-to-several, semi-detailed, serious, liberal.

Guthrie, Donald. *The Pastoral Epistles.* TNTC. Grand Rapids: Eerdmans, 1957. One-to-one, semi-detailed, serious, evangelical.

Hanson, A. T. *The Pastoral Epistles.* NCBC. Grand Rapids: Eerdmans, 1982. One-to-one, semi-detailed, technical, liberal.

Hendriksen, William. *Exposition of the Pastoral Epistles.* Grand Rapids: Baker, 1965. One-to-one, detailed, serious, evangelical.

———: see also 1 Thessalonians.

Houlden, J. L. *The Pastoral Epistles.* NTC. New York: Penguin, 1976; repr. Philadelphia: Trinity, 1989. One-to-one, detailed, technical, liberal.

Hultgren, Arland. *I Timothy, II Timothy, Titus.* ACNT. Minneapolis: Augsburg, 1984. One-to-several, detailed, serious, conservative-moderate.

Karris, Robert J., OFM. *The Pastoral Epistles.* NTM. Wilmington, DE: Michael Glazier, 1979. One-to-one, semi-detailed, serious, liberal.

Kelly, J. N. D. *A Commentary on the Pastoral Epistles.* HNTC. New
York: Harper and Row, 1963; repr. Grand Rapids: Baker, 1981;
repr. Peabody, MA: Hendrickson, 1987. One-to-one, detailed,
technical, conservative-moderate.

Kent, H. A. *The Pastoral Epistles: Studies in I and II Timothy and Titus.*
Chicago: Moody Press, 1958. One-to-one, detailed, popular,
evangelical.

Leaney, A. R. C. *The Epistles to Timothy, Titus, and Philemon.* TBC.
London: SCM, 1960. One-to-one, semi-detailed, serious, liberal.

Lock, W. *A Critical and Exegetical Commentary on the Pastoral
Epistles.* ICC. Edinburgh: T. & T. Clark, 1924. One-to-one,
in-depth, technical, liberal.

Moellering, H. A. *1 Timothy, 2 Timothy, Titus.* St. Louis: Concordia,
1970. One-to-one, detailed, serious, conervative-moderate.

Simpson, E. K. *The Pastoral Epistles: The Greek Text with Introduction
and Commentary.* Grand Rapids: Eerdmans, 1954. One-to-one,
detailed, technical, conservative-moderate.

Wilson, G. B. *The Pastoral Epistles.* Edinburgh: Banner of Truth,
1982. One-to-one, detailed, serious, evangelical.

2 Timothy

Barclay, W.: see 1 Timothy.

Barrett, C. K.: see 1 Timothy.

Bernard, J. H.: see 1 Timothy.

Blaiklock, E. M.: see 1 Timothy.

Dibelius, Martin, and Conzelmann, Hans: see 1 Timothy.

Earle, Ralph. *2 Timothy.* EBC. Grand Rapids: Zondervan, 1978.
One-to-several, detailed, serious, evangelical.

Fee, Gordon: see 1 Timothy.

Gealy, Fred: see 1 Timothy.

Guthrie, Donald: see 1 Timothy.

Hanson, A. T.: see 1 Timothy.

Hendriksen, William: see 1 Thessalonians and 1 Timothy.

Houlden, J. L.: see 1 Timothy.

Hultgren, Arland: see 1 Timothy.

Karris, Robert: see 1 Timothy.

Kelly, J. N. D.: see 1 Timothy.

Kent, H. A.: see 1 Timothy.

Leaney, A. R. C.: see 1 Timothy.

Lock, W.: see 1 Timothy.

Moellering, H. A.: see 1 Timothy.

Simpson, E. K.: see 1 Timothy.

Stott, John R. W. *The Message of 2 Timothy.* TBST. Leicester, England; Downers Grove, IL: InterVarsity, 1988. One-to-one, semi-detailed, serious, evangelical.

Wilson, G. B.: see 1 Timothy.

Titus

Barclay, W.: see 1 Timothy.

Barrett, C. K.: see 1 Timothy.

Bernard, J. H.: see 1 Timothy.

Blaiklock, E. M.: see 1 Timothy.

Dibelius, Martin, and Conzelmann, Hans: see 1 Timothy.

Fee, Gordon: see 1 Timothy.

Gealy, Fred. *Titus.* IB. Nashville: Abingdon, 1952. One-to-several, semi-detailed, technical, liberal.

Guthrie, Donald.: see 1 Timothy.

Hanson, A.T.: see 1 Timothy.

Hendriksen, William: see 1 Thessalonians and 1 Timothy.

Hiebert, D. Edmond. *Titus and Philemon.* Everyman's Bible Commentary Series. Chicago: Moody Press, 1957. One-to-one, semi-detailed, popular, evangelical.

————. *Titus.* EBC. Grand Rapids: Zondervan, 1978. One-to-several, detailed, serious, evangelical.

Houlden, J. L.: see 1 Timothy.

Hultgren, Arland: see 1 Timothy.

Karris, Robert: see 1 Timothy.

Kelly, J. N. D.: see 1 Timothy.

Kent, H. A.: see 1 Timothy.

Leaney, A. R. C.: see 1 Timothy.

Lock, W.: see 1 Timothy.

Moellering, H. A.: see 1 Timothy.

Simpson, E. K.: see 1 Timothy.

Wilson, G. B.: see 1 Timothy.

Philemon

Bruce, F. F.: see Colossians.

Caird, George B.: see Ephesians.

Carson, H. M.: see Colossians.

Getty, Mary Ann: see Philippians.
Hendriksen, William: see Philippians.
Hiebert, D. Edmond: see Titus.
Houlden, J. Leslie: see Philippians.
Knox, John. *Philemon.* IB. Nashville: Abingdon, 1952. One-to-several, semi-detailed, technical, liberal.
Lohse, E.: see Colossians.
Lucas, R. C.: see Colossians.
Martin, Ralph P.: see Colossians.
McDonald, H. Dermot: see Colossians.
Moule, C. F. D.: see Colossians.
Müller, J. J.: see Philippians.
Rupprecht, Arthur. *Philemon.* EBC. Grand Rapids: Zondervan, 1978. One-to-several, detailed, serious, evangelical.
Vaughan, Curtis: see Colossians.
Vincent, M. R.: see Philippians.
Wright, N. T.: see Colossians.

Hebrews

Attridge, Harold W. *Hebrews.* HERM. Philadelphia: Fortress, 1989. One-to-one, in-depth, technical, liberal.
Bowman, J. W. *Hebrews, James, I & II Peter.* LBC. Atlanta: John Knox, 1963. One-to-several, semi-detailed, popular, liberal.
Brown, Raymond. *The Message of Hebrews.* TBST. Leicester, England; Downers Grove, IL: InterVarsity, 1982. One-to-one, semi-detailed, serious, evangelical.
Bruce, F. F. *The Book of Hebrews.* NICNT. Grand Rapids: Eerdmans, 1964. One-to-one, in-depth, technical, evangelical.
Casey, Juliana, IHM. *Hebrews.* NTM. Wilmington, DE: Michael Glazier, 1980. One-to-one, semi-detailed, serious, liberal.
Guthrie, Donald. *The Epistle to the Hebrews.* TNTC. Grand Rapids: Eerdmans, 1983. One-to-one, detailed, serious, evangelical.
Kent, Homer A., Jr. *The Epistle to the Hebrews.* Grand Rapids: Baker, 1972. One-to-one, semi-detailed, technical, evangelical.
Kistemaker, Simon. *Hebrews.* Grand Rapids: Baker, 1984. One-to-one, semi-in-depth, serious, evangelical.
Moffatt, J. *A Critical and Exegetical Commentary on the Epistle to the Hebrews.* ICC. Edinburgh: T. & T. Clark, 1924. One-to-one, in-depth, technical, liberal.

Morris, Leon. *Hebrews*. BSC. Grand Rapids: Zondervan, 1986. One-to-one, semi-detailed, popular, evangelical.
————. *Hebrews*. EBC. Grand Rapids: Zondervan, 1981. One-to-several, detailed, serious, evangelical.
Purdy, Alexander. *Hebrews*. IB. Nashville: Abingdon, 1952. One-to-several, semi-detailed, technical, liberal.
Smith, Robert H. *Hebrews*. ACNT. Minneapolis: Augsburg, 1984. One-to-one, detailed, serious, conservative-moderate.
Wilson, R. McLellan. *Hebrews*. NCBC. Grand Rapids: Eerdmans, 1987. One-to-one, semi-detailed, technical, liberal.

James

Adamson, James B. *The Epistle of James*. NICNT. Eerdmans, 1976. One-to-one, in-depth, technical, evangelical.
Barclay, W. *The Letters of James and Peter*. DSB. Philadelphia: Westminster, 1960. One-to-one, semi-detailed, popular, conservative-moderate.
Blackman, E. C. *The Epistle of James*. TBC. London: SCM, 1947. One-to-one, semi-detailed, serious, liberal.
Bowman, J. W.: see Hebrews.
Burdick, Donald. *James*. EBC. Grand Rapids: Zondervan, 1981. One-to-several, detailed, serious, evangelical.
Davids, Peter H. *Commentary on James*. NIGTC. Grand Rapids: Eerdmans, 1982. One-to-one, in-depth, technical, conservative-moderate.
Dibelius, Martin, and Greeven, H. *James*. HERM. Philadelphia: Fortress, 1976. One-to-one, in-depth, technical, liberal.
Easton, Burton. *Introduction and Commentary to the Epistle of James*. IB. Nashville: Abingdon, 1952. One-to-several, semi-detailed, technical, liberal.
Hiebert, D. E. *The Epistle of James: Tests of a Living Faith*. Chicago: Moody Press, 1979. One-to-one, semi-detailed, popular, evangelical.
Hubbard, D. A. *The Book of James: Wisdom That Works*. Waco, TX: Word Books, 1980. One-to-one, semi-detailed, popular, evangelical.
Kent, Homer A., Jr. *Faith That Works: Studies in the Epistle of James*. Grand Rapids: Baker, 1986. One-to-one, detailed, serious, evangelical.

Kistemaker, Simon. *New Testament Commentary: Exposition of the Epistle of James and the Epistles of John.* Grand Rapids: Baker, 1986. One-to-one, semi-detailed, serious, evangelical.

Kugelman, Richard. *James and Jude.* NTM. Wilmington, DE: Michael Glazier, 1980. One-to-one, semi-detailed, serious, liberal.

Laws, Sophie. *A Commentary on the Epistle of James.* HNTC. New York: Harper and Row, 1980. One-to-one, detailed, serious, liberal.

Martin, R. A. *James.* Minneapolis: Augsburg, 1982. One-to-several, detailed, serious, conservative-moderate.

Martin, Ralph P. *James.* WBC. Waco, TX: Word Books, 1988. One-to-one, in-depth, technical, conservative-moderate.

Mayor, J. B. *The Epistle of St. James: The Greek Text with Introduction, Notes, and Comments.* Repr. Grand Rapids: Zondervan, 1954. One-to-one, detailed, technical, evangelical.

Mitton, C. L. *The Epistle of James.* Grand Rapids: Eerdmans, 1966. One-to-one, detailed, serious, conservative-moderate.

Moo, Douglas. *James.* TNTC. Grand Rapids: Eerdmans, 1987. One-to-one, detailed, serious, evangelical.

Motyer, J. A. *The Message of James.* TBST. Downers Grove, IL: Inter-Varsity, 1985. One-to-one, semi-detailed, serious, evangelical.

Reicke, Bo. *The Epistles of James, Peter, and Jude.* AB. Garden City: Doubleday, 1964. One-to-one, in-depth, technical, conservative-moderate.

Ropes, J. H. *St. James.* ICC. Edinburgh: T. & T. Clark, 1916. One-to-one, in-depth, technical, liberal.

Ross, A. *The Epistles of James and John.* NICNT. Grand Rapids: Eerdmans, 1954. One-to-one, in-depth, technical, evangelical.

Scaer, D. P. James, *The Apostle of Faith: A Primary Christological Document for the Persecuted Church.* St. Louis: Concordia, 1983. One-to-one, detailed, technical, conservative-moderate.

Sidebottom, E. M. *James, Jude, and 2 Peter.* NCBC. Grand Rapids: Eerdmans, 1967. One-to-one, semi-detailed, technical, liberal.

Tasker, R. V. G. *The General Epistle of James.* TNTC. Grand Rapids: Eerdmans, 1957. One-to-one, detailed, serious, evangelical.

Vaughan, Curtis. *James.* BSC. Grand Rapids: Zondervan, 1969. One-to-one, semi-detailed, popular, evangelical.

Williams, R. R.: see 1 John.

1 Peter

Beare, F. W. *The First Epistle of Peter: The Greek Text with Introduction and Notes.* 3d ed. Oxford: Blackwell, 1970. One-to-one, in-depth, technical, liberal.

Best, Ernest. *1 Peter.* NCBC. Grand Rapids: Eerdmans, 1982. One-to-one, semi-detailed, technical, liberal.

Bigg, C. *A Critical and Exegetical Commentary on the Epistles of St. Peter and St. Jude.* 2d ed. ICC. Edinburgh: T. & T. Clark, 1910. One-to-one, in-depth, technical, liberal.

Blum, Edwin. *1 Peter.* EBC. Grand Rapids: Zondervan, 1981. One-to-several, detailed, serious, evangelical.

Bowman, J. W.: see Hebrews.

Clowney, Edmund. *The Message of 1 Peter.* TBST. Leicester, England; Downers Grove, IL: InterVarsity, 1989. One-to-one, semi-detailed, serious, evangelical.

Cranfield, C. E. B. *I & II Peter and Jude.* TBC. London: SCM, 1960. One-to-one, semi-detailed, serious, liberal.

Elliott, John. *I Peter, II Peter, Jude.* ACNT. Minneapolis: Augsburg, 1982. One-to-several, detailed, serious, conservative-moderate.

Grudem, Wayne. *1 Peter.* Rev. ed. TNTC. Grand Rapids: Eerdmans, 1988. One-to-one, detailed, serious, evangelical.

Hiebert, D. Edmond. *First Peter: An Expositional Commentary.* Chicago: Moody Press, 1984. One-to-one, detailed, serious, evangelical.

Hunter, Archibald. *I Peter.* IB. Nashville: Abingdon, 1952. One-to-several, semi-detailed, technical, liberal.

Kelley, J. N. D. *A Commentary on the Epistles of Peter and Jude.* HNTC. New York: Harper and Row, 1969. One-to-one, detailed, technical, evangelical.

Kistemaker, Simon. *Expositions of the Epistles of Peter and Jude.* Grand Rapids: Baker, 1987. One-to-several, semi-detailed, serious, evangelical.

Leaney, R. C. *The Letters of Peter and Jude.* CBC. Cambridge: Cambridge University Press, 1967. One-to-one, semi-detailed, serious, liberal.

Michaels, J. Ramsey. *1 Peter.* WBC. Waco, TX: Word Books, 1988. One-to-one, in-depth, technical, conservative-moderate.

Mounce, Robert. *A Living Hope: A Commentary on First and Second Peter.* Grand Rapids: Eerdmans, 1982. One-to-one, detailed, serious, evangelical.

Reicke, Bo: see James.

Selwyn, E. G. *The First Epistle of Peter.* 2d ed. London: Macmillan, 1947. Repr. Grand Rapids: Baker, 1981. One-to-one, in-depth, technical, conservative-moderate.

Senior, Donald, CP. *1 and 2 Peter.* NTM. Wilmington, DE: Michael Glazier, 1980. One-to-one, semi-detailed, serious, liberal.

Vaughan, Curtis, and Lea, Thomas. *1, 2 Peter, Jude.* BSC. Grand Rapids: Zondervan, 1988. One-to-one, semi-detailed, popular, evangelical.

2 Peter

Barnett, Albert E. *The Second Epistle of Peter.* IB. Nashville: Abingdon, 1957. One-to-several, semi-detailed, technical, liberal.

Bigg, C.: see 1 Peter.

Blum, Edwin. *2 Peter.* EBC. Grand Rapids: Zondervan, 1981. One-to-several, detailed, serious, evangelical.

Bowman, J. W.: see Hebrews.

Cranfield, C. E. B.: see 1 Peter.

Elliott, John: see 1 Peter.

Green, Michael. *The Second Epistle General of Peter and the General Epistle of Jude.* Rev. ed. TNTC. Grand Rapids: Eerdmans, 1988. One-to-one, detailed, serious, evangelical.

Kelley, K. N. D.: see 1 Peter.

Kistemaker, Simon: see 1 Peter.

Leaney, A. R. C.: see 1 Peter.

Mounce, Robert: see 1 Peter.

Reicke, Bo: see James.

Senior, Donald: see 1 Peter.

Sidebottom, E. M.: see James.

Vaughan, Curtis, and Lea, Thomas: see 1 Peter.

1 John

Alexander, J. N. S. *The Epistles of John.* TBC. London: SCM, 1962. One-to-one, semi-detailed, serious, liberal.

Barker, C. J. *The Johannine Epistles.* London: Lutterworth Press, 1948. One-to-one, detailed, serious, conservative-moderate.

Barker, Glenn. *1 John.* EBC. Grand Rapids: Zondervan, 1981. One-to-several, detailed, serious, evangelical.

Brooke, A. E. *A Critical and Exegetical Commentary on the Johannine*

Epistles. ICC. Edinburgh: T. & T. Clark, 1912. One-to-one, in-depth, technical, liberal.

Brown, Raymond E. *The Epistles of John.* AB. Garden City: Doubleday, 1982. One-to-one, in-depth, technical, liberal.

Bruce, F. F. *The Epistles of John.* Old Tappan, NJ: Revell, 1970. One-to-one, detailed, serious, evangelical.

Bultmann, Rudolph. *The Johannine Epistles.* HERM. Philadelphia: Fortress, 1973. One-to-one, in-depth, technical, liberal.

Grayston, Kenneth. *The Johannine Epistles.* NCBC. Grand Rapids: Eerdmans, 1984. One-to-one, detailed, serious, liberal.

Houlden, J. L. *A Commentary on the Johannine Epistles.* New York: Harper and Row, 1973. One-to-one, detailed, serious, liberal.

Jackman, David. *The Message of John's Letters.* TBST. Leicester, England; Downers Grove, IL: InterVarsity, 1989. One-to-one, semi-detailed, serious, evangelical.

Kistemaker, Simon: see James.

Kysar, Robert. *I, II, III John.* ACNT. Minneapolis: Augsburg, 1987. One-to-one, detailed, serious, conservative-moderate.

Marshall, I. Howard. *The Epistles of John.* NICNT. Grand Rapids: Eerdmans, 1978. One-to-one, in-depth, technical, evangelical.

Perkins, Pheme. *The Johannine Epistles.* NTM. Wilmington, DE: Michael Glazier, 1979. One-to-one, semi-detailed, serious, liberal.

Smalley, Stephen S. *1, 2, 3 John.* WBC. Waco, TX: Word Books, 1984. One-to-one, in-depth, technical, conservative-moderate.

Stott, John R. W. *The Epistles of John.* TNTC. Grand Rapids: Eerdmans, 1964. One-to-one, semi-detailed, serious, evangelical.

Vaughan, Curtis. *1, 2, 3 John.* BSC. Grand Rapids: Zondervan, 1970. One-to-one, semi-detailed, popular, evangelical.

Wilder, Amos. *Introduction and Exegesis of I, II, and III John.* IB. Nashville: Abingdon, 1957. One-to-several, semi-detailed, technical, liberal.

Williams, R. R. *The Letters of John and James.* CBCNEB. Cambridge: Cambridge University Press, 1965. One-to-one, semi-detailed, serious, liberal.

2 John

Alexander, J. N. S.: see 1 John.
Barker, C. J.: see 1 John.

Barker, Glenn. *2 John.* EBC. Grand Rapids: Zondervan, 1981.
   One-to-several, detailed, serious, evangelical.
Brooke, A. E.: see 1 John.
Brown, Raymond: see 1 John.
Bruce, F. F.: see 1 John.
Bultmann, Rudolph: see 1 John.
Grayston, Kenneth: see 1 John.
Houlden, J. L.: see 1 John.
Jackman, David: see 1 John.
Kistemaker, Simon: see James.
Kysar, Robert: see 1 John.
Marshall, I. Howard: see 1 John.
Perkins, Pheme: see 1 John.
Smalley, Stephen S.: see 1 John.
Stott, John R. W.: see 1 John.
Vaughan, Curtis: see 1 John.
Wilder, Amos: see 1 John.
Williams, R. R.: see 1 John.

3 John

Alexander, J. N. S.: see 1 John.
Barker, C. J.: see 1 John.
Barker, Glenn. *3 John.* EBC. Grand Rapids: Zondervan, 1981.
   One-to-several, detailed, serious, evangelical.
Brooke, A. E.: see 1 John.
Brown, Raymond: see 1 John.
Bruce, F. F.: see 1 John.
Bultmann, Rudolph: see 1 John.
Grayston, Kenneth: see 1 John.
Houlden, J. L.: see 1 John.
Jackman, David: see 1 John.
Kistemaker, Simon: see James.
Kysar, Robert: see 1 John.
Marshall, I. Howard: see 1 John.
Perkins, Pheme: see 1 John.
Smalley, Stephen S.: see 1 John.
Stott, R. W.: see 1 John.
Vaughan, Curtis: see 1 John.
Wilder, Amos: see 1 John.
Williams, R. R.: see 1 John.

Jude

Barnett, Albert E. *The Epistle of Jude*. IB. Nashville: Abingdon, 1957. One-to-several, semi-detailed, technical, liberal.

Bauckham, Richard. *Jude, 2 Peter*. WBC. Waco, TX: Word Books, 1983. One-to-one, in-depth, technical, liberal.

Bigg, J.: see 1 Peter.

Blum, Edwin. *Jude*. EBC. Grand Rapids: Zondervan, 1981. One-to-several, detailed, serious, evangelical.

Cranfield, C. E. B.: see 1 Peter.

Elliott, John: see 1 Peter.

Green, Michael: see 2 Peter.

Kelly, J. N. D.: see 1 Peter.

Kistemaker, Simon: see 1 Peter.

Kugelman, Richard: see James.

Lawlor, G. L. *Translation and Exposition of the Epistle of Jude*. Nutley, NJ: Presbyterian and Reformed, 1976. One-to-one, semi-detailed, serious, evangelical.

Leaney, A. R. C.: see 1 Peter.

Reicke, Bo: see James.

Sidebottom, E. M.: see James.

Vaughan, Curtis and Lea, Thomas: see 1 Peter.

Revelation

Beasley-Murray, G. R. *The Book of Revelation*. Rev. ed. NCBC. Grand Rapids: Eerdmans, 1981;. One-to-one, semi-detailed, serious, evangelical.

Beckwith, I. T. *The Apocalypse of St. John*. Repr. Grand Rapids: Baker, 1967. One-to-one, in-depth, technical, conservative-moderate.

Boring, M. Eugene. *Revelation*. INT. Louisville: John Knox, 1989. One-to-one, semi-detailed, serious, liberal.

Caird, George B. *The Revelation of St. John the Divine*. HNTC. New York: Harper and Row, 1966. One-to-one, detailed, serious, liberal.

Charles, R. H. *Revelation*. 2 vols. ICC. Edinburgh: T. & T. Clark, 1920. One-to-one, in-depth, technical, liberal.

Collins, Adela Yarbro. *The Apocalypse*. NTM. Wilmington, DE: Michael Glazier, 1979. One-to-one, semi-detailed, serious, liberal.

Corsini, Eugenio. *The Apocalypse*. Wilmington: Michael Glazier, 1983. One-to-one, detailed, serious, liberal.

Glasson, T. F. *The Revelation of John.* CBCNEB. New York: Cambridge University, 1965. One-to-one, semi-detailed, serious, liberal.

Hendriksen, William. *More Than Conquerors. An Interpretation of the Book of Revelation.* One-to-one, semi-detailed, serious, evangelical.

Johnson, Alan. *Revelation.* BSC. Grand Rapids: Zondervan, 1986. One-to-one, semi-detailed, popular, evangelical.

————. *Revelation.* EBC. Grand Rapids: Zondervan, 1981. One-to-one, detailed, serious, evangelical.

Kiddle, Martin. *The Revelation of St. John.* New York: Harper and Brothers, 1940. One-to-one, detailed, serious, liberal.

Krodel, Gerhard. *Revelation.* ACNT. Minneapolis: Augsburg Fortress, 1989. One-to-one, detailed, serious, liberal.

Ladd, George E. *A Commentary on the Revelation of John.* Grand Rapids: Eerdmans, 1972. One-to-one, detailed, serious, evangelical.

Morris, Leon. *Revelation.* Rev. ed. TNTC. Grand Rapids: Eerdmans, 1987. One-to-one, semi-detailed, serious, evangelical.

Mounce, Robert H. *The Book of Revelation.* NICNT. Eerdmans, 1977. One-to-one, in-depth, technical, evangelical.

Mulholland, Robert, Jr. *Revelation.* Grand Rapids: Zondervan, 1990. One-to-one, detailed, serious, evangelical.

Rist, Martin. *Revelation.* IB. Nashville: Abingdon, 1952. One-to-several, semi-detailed, technical, liberal.

Swete, H. B. *The Apocalypse of St. John.* 3d ed. London: Macmillan, 1911. One-to-one, in-depth, technical, liberal.

Wilcock, Michael. *The Message of Revelation.* TBST. Downers Grove, IL: InterVarsity, 1975. One-to-one, semi-detailed, popular, evangelical.

4

Selected Single-Volume (One-to-All) Commentaries

This listing contains only those single-volume commentaries that I consider to have a high overall degree of reliability. I have been rather stringent in this regard, because it is my opinion that almost all the readers of this book will want to start out in their commentary purchasing or borrowing by obtaining a commentary of this sort. Everyone who reads the Bible regularly would profit from owning one. You deserve to get a good one, and I have limited the list to those I know are produced by sound scholarship, regardless of theological slant. Even the liberal volumes don't have enough room to become all that skeptical of the text, so explication wins out over experimentation in those as well as in the consciously evangelical publications.

Evangelical Commentary on the Bible. Ed. Walter A. Elwell. Grand Rapids: Baker, 1989. One-to-all, summary, serious, evangelical. This new volume has only recently become available, and my sampling of it indicates that it deserves high praise and wide readership. It is written mostly by American evangelicals, is solidly evangelical in theology, and is more up-to-date than the comparable *Wycliffe Bible Commentary* which it is apparently destined to succeed, I would think.

Harper's Bible Commentary. Ed. James L. Mays, with the Society of Biblical Literature. New York: Harper and Row, 1988. One-to-all, summary, serious, liberal. Among the liberal one-volume commentaries, this and the *Jerome Biblical Commentary* are the best.

This volume covers the Apocrypha, has a bit more space than any of the others listed here, is authored by leading liberal scholars, mostly from the United States, and is by a slight margin the most skeptical-critical of the bunch.

The International Bible Commentary. Ed. F. F. Bruce. Rev. ed. Grand Rapids: Zondervan, 1986. One-to-all, summary, serious, evangelical. Based on a 1979 revision of the 1969 one-volume commentary called *A New Testament Commentary,* this fine volume contains comments on the biblical text by some of the English-speaking world's best scholars, and is edited by a master commentator. It closely rivals the *New Bible Commentary,* which it also resembles in several ways.

The Interpreter's One-Volume Commentary on the Bible. Ed. Charles M. Laymon. Nashville: Abingdon, 1971. One-to-all, summary, serious, liberal. This volume is a close runner-up in quality and usefulness to the *Harper's Bible Commentary* and the *Jerome Biblical Commentary.* I find it a bit less liberally slanted than the former and more than the latter, and somewhat more given to speculative discussion and less to explication of the text in a fashion most readers of this sort of commentary would actually be looking for.

The Jerome Biblical Commentary. Ed. Raymond E. Brown, Joseph Fitzmyer, S. J., and Roland E. Murphy, O. Carm. Englewood Cliffs, NJ: Prentice-Hall, 1968. One-to-all, summary, serious, liberal. This book is the product of distinguished, mostly liberal, Roman Catholic scholars, who have done a fine job of condensing a great deal of information into a relatively small space. It includes, of course, comments on the books of the Apocrypha, which are canonical in Roman Catholicism.

The New Bible Commentary, Revised. Ed. Donald Guthrie, et al. Grand Rapids: Eerdmans, 1970. One-to-all, summary, serious, evangelical. The product of British and American evangelicals, this is the standard against which all others must be compared. It more often illuminates the text in a judicious way than the others, and is already scheduled for a new, fully revised edition in the early 1990s.

Peake's Commentary on the Bible. Ed. Matthew Black and H. H. Rowley. Nashville: Thomas Nelson, 1962. One-to-all, summary, serious, liberal. Peake's has been around for several decades, and has thus gone through several revisions that have kept it up-to-date. Its individual portions are written mainly by liberal British scholars.

Wycliffe Bible Commentary. Ed. Charles F. Pfeiffer and Everett F. Harrison. Chicago: Moody Press, 1962. A team of top American evangelical scholars contributed to this volume, which, though now almost three decades old, is still highly usable and well worth owning. Like any of the others, it has places in which it is the very best of them all.

5

Major Commentary Series

Here we list only those commentary sets that also appear, on balance, to fit the criteria listed for individual volumes in chapter 3. A number of series have thus been excluded as either inferior in quality, so homiletically or devotionally oriented as not to address the biblical text in sufficient detail, or otherwise specialized, outdated, or unsatisfactory. There are a good many poor-quality volumes among the series listed here, but overall, these series are worthy of any Bible student's attention.

The Anchor Bible. Edited by William Foxwell Albright and David Noel Freedman; exclusively by Freedman since Albright's death. Garden City: Doubleday. This ecumenical series started out in the early 1960s as a new translation of the Bible with exegetical notes, but has evolved into a full commentary series including the Apocrypha. Separate volumes cover all but the shortest biblical books and the series is now about two-thirds complete. The older volumes (before about 1978) are semi-detailed or detailed; the newer volumes are in-depth. Nearly all are technical and theologically liberal, and most pay good attention to linguistic issues, if not to balanced exegesis.

The Augsburg Commentary on the New Testament. Minneapolis: Augsburg (now Augsburg Fortress). A partially conservative-moderate series with some liberal volumes, written mainly by Lutheran scholars. Most volumes are detailed and serious.

The Bible Study Commentary. Grand Rapids: Zondervan (Lamplighter Books). This series, covering the entire Bible, became complete in 1989. It is written mostly by less well known evangelical scholars in a popular vein, but with a sufficient degree of depth and good analysis of the text that it approaches being a "serious" commentary in some of its volumes. It is a fairly good choice for a beginner in the use of commentaries, especially in the case of a desire to study a given biblical book by itself (as in a home or church Bible class format) since most individual biblical books are treated in a separate paperback commentary of their own.

Broadman Bible Commentary. Edited by Clifton J. Allen et al. 12 vols. A series written by Southern Baptist scholars covering the entire Bible, completed in 1969. It varies in quality, but should not be overlooked as an occasionally valuable evangelical and conservative-moderate series. Little new ground is broken in this sort of series, and its blandness means that none of the volumes has been especially influential.

The Cambridge Bible Commentary on the New English Bible. Edited by Peter Ackroyd, A. R. C. Leaney, and J. W. Packer. New York and Cambridge: Cambridge University Press. This full series of biblical commentaries, mainly the product of British scholars, provides a standard and reliable, semi-detailed coverage of the biblical books from a moderate and liberal point of view. Most of its volumes were produced in the 1960s and 1970s.

Continental Commentaries. Minneapolis: Augsburg (now Augsburg Fortress). English translations of major, rather prestigious German Lutheran commentaries of fairly recent vintage (1960s–1980s). Nearly all volumes are liberal, in-depth, and technical.

The Daily Study Bible. OT edited by John C. L. Gibson. NT revision edited by C. L. Rawlins. Philadelphia: Westminster Press. A popular-level commentary series. The NT volumes were all authored by William Barclay in the 1950s and 1960s, and depend entirely on the level of his NT knowledge at any given point for their effectiveness. The OT volumes come from the 1980s, are not very detailed, and vary in quality, though written by recognized scholars, most of whom are liberal theologically. Barclay's NT volumes have always sold well, but the OT series, now complete, has been less well received. The Tyndale Old Testament Commentary, at half the price, is a much better buy.

Everyman's Bible Commentary. Chicago: Moody Press. This series is truly simple in its language and requires virtually no knowledge of the Bible to follow. It is for the beginner, providing a gentle introduction to the biblical text, and would not be of much interest to the pastor or serious Bible student with some knowledge of the Bible already in hand.

The Expositor's Bible Commentary. Edited by Frank E. Gaebelein et al. Grand Rapids: Zondervan. This is a twelve-volume series written by evangelical scholars of varying ability. As a result, each volume tends to have one or more superb commentaries bound with one or more weak ones. Nevertheless, it is a series that a pastor or teacher would probably consider worth owning. The introductory articles on various OT and NT topics are generally well written. The series is ongoing and nearing completion (the NT part is already finished), with a complete set likely available in the early 1990s.

Good News Commentaries. Edited by W. Ward Gasque. San Francisco: Harper and Row. A new series launched in the early 1980s, mostly complete, based on the text of the Good News Bible (Today's English Version), largely evangelical in character, presented in a format designed to appeal to intelligent lay people as well as students and pastors. The writers are capable evangelical or conservative scholars, and the volumes are either semi-detailed or detailed in length.

Harper's New Testament Commentaries. Edited by Henry Chadwick. New York: Harper and Row. This nearly finished series offers mainly mid-length (detailed) volumes on NT books, by recognized scholars, most of whom are British or American. The majority are either liberal or moderate. Good scholars have written for this series, providing in their volumes fresh translations. The commentaries are both readable and judicious in what they offer, for the most part, and do not require a knowledge of Greek to follow. Only one or two commentaries on Pauline epistles are yet to appear in the series.

Hermeneia: A Critical and Historical Commentary on the Bible. Edited by Frank Moore Cross, Jr., et al. (OT) and Helmut Koester, et al. (NT). Philadelphia: Fortress Press. This series, currently incomplete, aims to provide the best of liberal, technical scholarship in volumes that are in-depth, providing thorough bibliographical information as well. There is also an emphasis on providing parallel texts (i.e., literature from the ancient world that illuminates the Bible) although the way that this literature is allowed to influence biblical interpretation is not always convincing. Some reviewers have even criticized the series as suffering from "parallelomania." The editors have chosen some works already published (mainly from volumes originally in German and translated into English for this series) going back as far as the late 1950s, and have added both newly commissioned English commentaries and recent German commentaries in English translation. All the volumes are written by world-class scholars, though the quality varies as it does in any multi-volume series.

Interpreter's Bible. Edited by George A. Buttrick. Nashville: Abingdon Press, 1952–57. This is a classic American liberal commentary series from the 1950s, with several commentaries bound together in each volume. The only useful part is the Introduction and Exegesis for each book, usually written by a separate author from the one who wrote the "Exposition." Nearly all the homiletical "expositions" on each book are written by preachers rather than scholars, and are characterized by the worst sort of outdated liberal Protestant moralizing, universalizing, personalizing, and a host of other classic interpretational flaws, and are, ironically, not worth consulting except for examples of how *not* to interpret the Bible. The series is especially marred by its brevity, so much space being taken up by the expositions.

The International Critical Commentary. Edited currently by J. A. Emerton, et al. Edinburgh: T. & T. Clark. This highly technical series went into production in the 1880s and continued through the 1920s, never being completed (a few biblical books are not covered). The scholars who wrote for it were some of the best of their day, and it therefore is a series still well worth owning. Along with Keil and Delitzsch, it is the oldest series I list in this book, but the quality was and remains high (some of the volumes being the best liberal volumes still available on given biblical books!). There is now a revision underway, and new volumes will be produced to replace those that have become more dated than the others, or to fill holes that the incomplete series left in coverage of the biblical text. It is noteworthy for its thoroughness and technical depth. In some of the volumes, the theology is so minimal that a reader of any theological persuasion can actually employ the commentary quite profitably—though of course without learning much about the given book's theology. Those who cannot read Hebrew, Greek, and Latin will find it hard to use.

Interpretation: A Bible Commentary for Teaching and Preaching. Edited by James L. Mays. Atlanta: John Knox (more recently Louisville: Westminster/John Knox). Here is a mostly liberal, mid-length commentary series of generally good quality, rather recently underway with volumes appearing currently, and about a fourth of the projected total in print. The emphasis is less on consistent exegesis than on analysis of themes and perspectives, a somewhat risky approach since only thorough exegesis can undergird theological analysis convincingly.

International Theological Commentary. Grand Rapids: Eerdmans. A new series, with just a few volumes so far published, composed partly of translations from European works. In spite of its name, this series has no corner on theology, and some of the volumes that have appeared so far are actually not even especially theological in emphasis. The theology represented is largely liberal.

Keil and Delitzsch, Old Testament Commentaries. By Carl F. Keil and Franz Delitzsch. Grand Rapids: Eerdmans. Known everywhere simply as Keil and Delitzsch, this series of two dozen volumes covers the entire OT. Even though these volumes were originally written in the nineteenth century, and even though all the volumes are the product of one or the other or both of the two authors, there's still nothing in print quite like Keil and Delitzsch. Here were two scholars who really knew the OT and put many years into its careful exposition. This series is for the well-trained OT student. Those who do not know Hebrew and Greek and cannot read Latin will find much of it over their heads.

The Layman's Bible Book Commentary. 24 vols. Nashville: Broadman Press, completed in 1984. A complete set of commentaries, all relatively brief and popular in level, the product of Southern Baptist scholars. Nearly all the volumes are conservative in theology, though some authors thinly disguise their more liberal views by carefully hedging their remarks.

Layman's Bible Commentary. 25 vols. Atlanta: John Knox (now Louisville: Westminster/John Knox). Edited by B. H. Kelly, et al. An older series, begun in the late 1950s and still ongoing, some of the volumes of which are out of print now. Most of the volumes are by liberals, and the target audience is lay people. Capable scholars wrote the volumes, and they occasionally offer useful insight, although at a surface level. The series as a whole is unimpressive, and much better coverage of the text is provided in, for example, the Tyndale series.

New Century Bible Commentary. Currently edited by Ronald E. Clements (OT) and Matthew Black (NT). Grand Rapids: Eerdmans; London: Marshall, Morgan and Scott. A series that started in the 1950s with the name New Century Bible, whose volumes vary widely in quality and length, although each is written by a capable scholar. The aim of the series is to provide critical attention to the text itself without paying too much attention to other issues. The overall theological stance is liberal. Only some of the volumes are noteworthy. The later volumes vary somewhat in depth of coverage, but are either in-depth or detailed.

The New Clarendon Bible. A British series that died about a decade ago, understandably, after just a few of its mostly brief and undistinguished volumes appeared. Nevertheless, it contained a few valuable commentaries.

The New International Bible Commentary. Peabody, MA: Hendrickson Publishers. A new evangelical series based on the NIV and aimed at sound scholarship and fairly in-depth treatment of the biblical books. Only one volume is yet released in this series (Fee's volume on the Pastoral Epistles). The series has high potential, even though produced by a small publisher.

New International Commentary on the New Testament. Edited by F. F. Bruce. Grand Rapids: Eerdmans. This series has been underway since the 1950s and contains among its volumes some of the best evangelical NT scholarship—or scholarship, period—available. The series is about 85 percent complete now, and some of the older volumes are either being revised or replaced. Bruce, the editor, has himself written commentaries on every book of the NT (not in this series, of course) and he knows how to pick and give editorial guidance to good authors. The series is especially characterized by its even quality: There are not many poor volumes in the mix. It requires no knowledge of Greek to follow the comments, although the footnotes do contain Greek or other languages frequently.

New International Commentary on the Old Testament. Edited by R. K. Harrison. Grand Rapids: Eerdmans. Like the NICNT this series provides rather high quality evangelical and conservative scholarship on the OT books and is something of a standard for evangelical scholarship. Most of the volumes are not as technical as those in, for example, the Word Biblical Commentary (though some are even more so), but theological stance and overall quality are more predictable. The series is nearing the halfway point in completion, and some of its volumes are to be considered best buys.

New International Greek Testament Commentary. Edited by I. Howard Marshall. Grand Rapids: Eerdmans. A new series, begun in the late 1970s, with just a few commentaries yet in print, that will, if the established pattern continues, result in the most in-depth, technical coverage of the NT books in a full series. That such a series should be evangelical in theology is a plus for all who are interested in serious NT exposition.

New Testament Commentaries. Edited by Howard Clark Kee and Dennis Nineham. Philadelphia: Trinity Press International. A new series just underway from an Episcopalian publishing house, edited by two fine scholars, that promises to bring high-quality volumes to publication.

New Testament Message. A Biblical-Theological Commentary. Edited by Wilfred Harrington, OP, and Donald Senior, SJ. Wilmington, DE: Michael Glazier. This series provides volumes that are only semi-detailed, but offers nevertheless a kind of distillation of capable Roman Catholic liberal scholarship on the Bible. The goal of the series is to provide modern preachers and teachers with an understanding of the message of the biblical text rather than details about exegetical matters. Some volumes do this better than others.

The Old Testament Library. Originally edited by G. Ernest Wright, et al., and more recently by Peter Ackroyd, et al. Philadelphia: Westminster Press. The OTL is a major Old Testament commentary series, still half incomplete, begun in the 1950s, with some volumes already out of print. Some of its volumes represent the best of liberal American Protestant scholarship; others are run-of-the-mill. These volumes are almost all in-depth but not technical, so they are accessible to almost any serious reader.

Old Testament Message. A Biblical-Theological Commentary. Edited by Carroll Stuhlmueller, CP, and Martin McNamara, MSC. Wilmington, DE: Michael Glazier. What is said above about the New Testament Message series generally applies to this series as well. They are designed to correspond to one another.

Pelican New Testament Commentaries. Some volumes published in London by Penguin Books, some by Penguin and SCM, some by Westminster Press in Philadelphia. A mixed commentary series, authored mostly by British scholars in the 1960s and 1970s. It contains some volumes that are notable for their clarity, sound scholarship, and careful attention to the text, but on the whole it has not been considered an influential or innovative series. Most volumes are liberal in theology; a few are conservative-moderate.

Text and Interpretation. A Practical Commentary. Edited by A. S. van der Woude. Grand Rapids: Eerdmans. A new series of moderately detailed, mostly liberal commentaries, many originally published in Europe and now translated into English. The series is, of course, only partially complete as yet. It presents to the reader a selection of commentaries chosen for their application rather than strictly for their exegetical depth.

Torch Bible Commentaries. London: SCM. Edited by John Marsh. A series of quite brief commentaries on the biblical text (with a few longer exceptions) authored mainly by British scholars who concentrate on exegetical issues, with some attention to theology as well. These commentaries' brevity is both their strength and their disadvantage, depending on how much depth a given passage requires for proper coverage. The series, begun in the late 1950s, was completed in the 1960s.

The Bible Speaks Today. Edited by J. A. Motyer (OT) and John R. W. Stott (NT). Leicester, England; Downers Grove, IL: InterVarsity. A new evangelical commentary series written for the serious Bible student, emphasizing sound scholarship combined with intelligent interpretation. No detailed, original-language exegesis or substantial interaction with secondary literature are found in this series, but its volumes so far indicate a sound, useful set will eventuate. A good many of the volumes that have appeared so far are revisions, to a greater or lesser degree, of sound, evangelical commentaries published in the past by InterVarsity.

Tyndale New Testament Commentaries. Revision edited by Leon Morris. Grand Rapids: Eerdmans. Separate volumes on all but the shortest NT books. Most volumes are semi-detailed in length of discussion and serious in level. Nearly all are evangelical. It's an awfully good series for the money, and the one complete multi-volume NT series that any pastor or Bible student at any level could invest in without fear that it would not receive regular use over the years.

Tyndale Old Testament Commentaries. Edited by Donald J. Wiseman. Some volumes published in Grand Rapids by Eerdmans; some by InterVarsity in Downers Grove, IL. Separate volumes on all but the shortest OT books. Most of the volumes are semi-detailed, and all are serious in level. Nearly all are evangelical; a few volumes in some aspects are conservative-moderate. For the general reader, this series is hard to beat. The authors are mostly British, erudite, and write very clearly. The series is just a few volumes away from completion (twenty-one of twenty-five are available), and has to be considered a best buy.

The Wesleyan Bible Commentary. Edited by Charles W. Carter. 6 vols. Repr. Peabody, MA: Hendrickson, 1986. This series offers evangelical, semi-detailed commentaries on all the biblical books, written by scholars who are in the Wesleyan-Arminian theological tradition. The commentaries are not actually affected by the stance of the writers any more than the volumes in any other series would be, and the set provides generally sound, if not terribly detailed, explication of the text.

Word Biblical Commentary. Edited by David Hubbard and Glenn Barker. Dallas: Word Books. Separate volumes on all but the shortest biblical books. In-depth, technical volumes, some conservative-moderate, some evangelical, and not a few liberal, even though Word itself is an evangelical publisher and the series is called "the best in evangelical critical scholarship." This series is notable for its excellent format, thorough bibliographical information, and overall quality, in spite of the wide theological range. It provides commentary at a high level technically, yet foreign language material is translated for the non-specialist. It is about as thorough in detail as any series available. Some of its volumes are better than anything else in print. The series is now about half complete.

6

The Very Best Commentaries

To repeat, the basic rule of commentary use is: *Always consult more than one commentary*. It is entirely unlikely that any single author can produce a commentary that will be fully balanced, fully comprehensive, and fully accurate. Nevertheless, that doesn't mean that we cannot identify those commentaries that come closest to the ideal within the obvious limitations that apply to every commentary.

In this chapter we list what are in our judgment (1) the best single-volume commentary; (2) the best series; (3) the best individual commentaries on single books of the Bible. A listing like this is certainly somewhat subjective, and clearly dependent on criteria that not everyone will agree with. However, the process of selection of commentaries must be done by those whose funds and time are limited—i.e., all of us. Neither we nor even the most prestigious libraries are in a position to purchase every commentary. And no one has the time to read them all. Here, then, are our picks.

Best Single-Volume Bible Commentary

The New Bible Commentary, Revised. Ed. Donald Guthrie, et al. Downers Grove, IL: InterVarsity, 1970. Others are good, but this one has the best scholarship overall (mainly leading British and American evangelical scholars) and a high degree of consistency in quality. Like any of the one-volume commentaries, it's summary in scope and non-technical.

Best Commentary Series

Technical, in-depth, and complete, Old Testament:

Keil and Delitzsch. **Commentary on the Old Testament** (Grand Rapids: Eerdmans). There are so few technical, in-depth OT commentaries that are complete that Keil and Delitzsch walks away with the prize somewhat by default. For evangelicals, this series is a real plus, because it is solidly respectful of scriptural accuracy throughout.

Serious, detailed, and nearly complete, Old Testament:

The Tyndale Old Testament Commentary (Grand Rapids: Eerdmans; and Downers Grove, IL: InterVarsity). One could hardly go wrong purchasing this set. With the exception of three OT books, it's complete, and it is readable, properly cautious, scholarly while not technical, and a nice combination of exegesis and theological reflection.

Serious, detailed / in depth, and complete, New Testament:

The New International Commentary on the New Testament (NICNT; Grand Rapids: Eerdmans). This commentary series is not as technical as the two listed above, nor as typically in-depth in coverage (though some of its volumes are a match for any in thoroughness), but it has the virtue of being complete and, in fact, some of its less well received volumes are being replaced by newer works intended to update and strengthen the series.

Technical, in-depth, and partially complete, New Testament:

Here there is a tie between the **Word Biblical Commentary** (formerly Waco, TX; now Dallas: Word Books) and the **New International Greek Testament Commentary** (Grand Rapids: Eerdmans). The latter is more consistently conservative in theology; the former varies considerably. Both series are characterized by great depth of analysis and a high level of interaction with the scholarly literature on the various NT books.

Best Commentaries on Individual Books of the Bible

Genesis

Baldwin, Joyce. **The Message of Genesis 12–50**. TBST. Leicester, England; Downers Grove, IL: InterVarsity, 1988. This serious, evangelical work is another triumph for Baldwin, who hasn't yet written a bad commentary.

Kidner, Derek. *Genesis.* TOTC. Downers Grove, IL: InterVarsity, 1967. Here is another serious, evangelical commentary that comes from a distinguished British OT scholar whose books are all characterized by judgment and overall competence.

Wenham, Gordon. *Genesis 1–15.* WBC. Waco, TX: Word Books, 1987. Wenham's in-depth, technical commentary is also evangelical in theology, and the most judicious of the Genesis commentaries written at a technical level. Wenham is a sort of Pentateuch specialist among commentators and his second volume in the WBC series (Genesis 16–50) will probably be every bit as good as this one.

Exodus

Childs, Brevard. *The Book of Exodus: A Critical, Theological Commentary.* OTL. Louisville: Westminster/John Knox, 1962. This technical, liberal commentary pays attention to the final form of the text, in comparison to most liberal commentaries on the Pentateuchal books, and it is written by a scholar who really knows his stuff.

Kaiser, Walter, Jr. *Exodus.* EBC. Grand Rapids: Zondervan, 1989. A carefully done, rather brief, serious, evangelical commentary limited by being bound with some weaker commentaries in the same volume.

Leviticus

Wenham, Gordon. *The Book of Leviticus.* NICOT. Grand Rapids: Eerdmans, 1979. Here is a somewhat in-depth, technical, evangelical volume on a difficult book and as a commentary on Leviticus it has no serious rival.

Numbers

Wenham, Gordon. *Numbers.* TOTC. Downers Grove, IL: InterVarsity, 1982. Wenham's detailed, serious, evangelical commentary on Numbers is the third of our picks from this author in just four OT books. But there's nothing better on Numbers.

Deuteronomy

Craigie, Peter. *The Book of Deuteronomy.* NICOT. Grand Rapids: Eerdmans, 1976. An in-depth, technical, evangelical volume that takes seriously the early date of Deuteronomy and relates the book well to the rest of Scripture.

Wright, G. Ernest. *Deuteronomy*. IB. Nashville: Abingdon, 1952. A semi-detailed, liberal volume bound with some duds, but a careful analysis of Deuteronomy by one of the best liberal, theologically astute OT scholars of the postwar era.

Joshua

✓ Woudstra, Marten H. *The Book of Joshua*. NICOT. Grand Rapids: Eerdmans, 1981. Woudstra's commentary is fairly in-depth, evangelical, and serious about making sense of a book that requires delicate historical and archaeological analysis.

Judges

Boling, Robert G. *Judges*. AB. Garden City: Doubleday, 1975. Boling's technical, liberal commentary is distinguished by its careful treatment of a book that has been somewhat neglected by commentators (at least by good ones).

✓ Cundall, Arthur E., and Morris, Leon. *Judges and Ruth*. TOTC. Grand Rapids: Eerdmans, 1968. This serious, evangelical commentary will help preachers and teachers better than any other.

Ruth

Atkinson, David. *The Message of Ruth*. TBST. Downers Grove, IL: InterVarsity, 1983. Atkinson's evangelical commentary is only semi-detailed, but he gets the theology down pretty well, and that's what's most important about understanding Ruth.

Hubbard, Robert L., Jr. *The Book of Ruth*. NICOT. Grand Rapids: Eerdmans, 1990. This is a brand-new, in-depth, technical, evangelical volume that will, I think, quickly supplant other longer, technical commentaries on the little gem of a book that it's written about.

1 Samuel

Klein, Ralph W. *1 Samuel*. WBC. Waco, TX: Word Books, 1983. Like all the volumes in the WBC, this one is in-depth and technical, and unlike some, also skeptical of the accuracy of the narrative in enough parts to be called liberal. Klein explains the textual issues better than anyone else (he's a first-rate OT text critic) and the format of the series forces him to include enough theology (usually lacking in commentaries on the historical books) that this volume is a genuine help to the serious student.

✓ Baldwin, Joyce G. *1 and 2 Samuel.* TOTC. Downers Grove, IL: InterVarsity, 1988. Baldwin's serious, evangelical commentary is another of her consistently successful efforts.

2 Samuel

McCarter, P. Kyle. *2 Samuel.* AB. Garden City: Doubleday, 1984. This careful commentary from a fine scholar is in-depth, technical, and liberal. It contains almost no theology to speak of and is thus often "neutral" enough to be of interest to both liberals and evangelicals.

Baldwin, Joyce G. *1 and 2 Samuel.* TOTC. Downers Grove, IL: InterVarsity, 1988. Even though only semi-detailed, this serious, evangelical commentary is the best to use if you are interested in the theological issues in 2 Samuel (as anyone ought to be).

1 Kings

DeVries, Simon J. *1 Kings.* WBC. Waco, TX: Word Books, 1985. There are not many notable commentaries on 1 Kings, and to say that this one is the best of them is not to praise it especially highly. It's in-depth, technical, and essentially liberal. The best thing about it is its interest in theological themes, although I'm not convinced these are always handled convincingly.

2 Kings

Hobbs, T. R. *2 Kings.* WBC. Waco, TX: Word Books, 1985. This in-depth, technical, conservative-moderate commentary is the best of a small field, written by a scholar who is genuinely competent, and concerned to fulfill the aims of the WBC series. In that regard it's not bad, but the last word on 2 Kings has hardly been written.

1 Chronicles

Braun, Roddy. *1 Chronicles.* WBC. Waco, TX: Word Books, 1986. Here's another basically liberal volume in a technical, in-depth series that was supposed to provide "the best of evangelical critical scholarship."

Payne, J. Barton. *1 and 2 Chronicles.* EBC. Grand Rapids: Zondervan, 1988. Payne's serious, evangelical volume is far from ideal, bound with some other commentaries not as impressive, and yet frequently very helpful.

2 Chronicles

Dillard, Raymond B. *2 Chronicles.* WBC. Waco, TX: Word Books, 1987. Dillard's in-depth, technical commentary is the product of much careful work, and is rated here conservative-moderate rather than evangelical mainly because he thinks the writer of Chronicles made up a portion of the material in the book.

Ezra and Nehemiah

Kidner, Derek. *Ezra and Nehemiah.* TOTC. Downers Grove, IL: InterVarsity, 1979. Here is another of Kidner's serious, evangelical contributions to the fine TOTC series.

Yamauchi, Edwin. *Ezra and Nehemiah.* EBC. Grand Rapids: Zondervan, 1988. Yamauchi is a great linguist and historian, and in a very good position to write this serious, evangelical commentary. To buy it, you must buy some commentaries bound with it that you may not value as much.

Esther

Baldwin, Joyce. *Esther.* TOTC. Downers Grove, IL: InterVarsity, 1984. Baldwin's serious, evangelical treatment of this book does not take the same interpretational paths I would in each case, but it's still a very fine treatment of the fascinating story of Jews adapting to a pagan culture.

Job

Smick, Elmer. *Job.* EBC. Grand Rapids: Zondervan, 1988. This detailed, serious, evangelical commentary is the product of a first-rate senior OT scholar whose views are judicious and thoroughly informed.

Clines, David J. A. *Job 1–20.* WBC. Dallas: Word Books, 1989. Clines' in-depth, technical, liberal commentary is so thorough it almost loses the reader, but it can't be beat for interaction with the scholarly literature and for analysis of every jot and tittle in the Book of Job (so far).

Psalms

Craigie, Peter. *Psalms 1–50.* WBC. Waco, TX: Word Books, 1983. Craigie's commentary is in-depth, technical, and evangelical, and the product of someone who really knew and understood the Psalms.

Kidner, Derek. *Psalms 1–72. Psalms 73–150.* TOTC. Downers Grove, IL: InterVarsity, 1973, 1975. These volumes are not as detailed as many others, but are serious, evangelical, and filled with much helpful insight.

Proverbs

Kidner, Derek. *Proverbs.* TOTC. Downers Grove, IL: InterVarsity, 1975. Kidner is well known for his work in the wisdom literature of the OT. This serious, evangelical commentary is only semi-detailed, so it hardly covers every proverb, but it teaches the reader about Proverbs better than any commentary I know.

Ecclesiastes

Kidner, Derek. *The Message of Ecclesiastes.* TBST. Downers Grove, IL: InterVarsity, 1988. This serious, evangelical commentary finds more positive, orthodox thinking in the book than this famous "theological foil" of the OT actually contains, but it's the best of its category.

Whybray, R. N. *Ecclesiastes.* NCBC. Grand Rapids: Eerdmans, 1989. Whybray's in-depth, technical, liberal commentary is up-to-date, thorough, and judicious.

Song of Songs

Carr, G. Lloyd. *The Song of Solomon.* TOTC. Downers Grove, IL: InterVarsity, 1984. Carr, an accomplished dramatist as well as OT scholar, has written a serious, evangelical commentary that pays proper attention to the genre of the Song, and among other things contains a convincing refutation of the sometimes-advanced idea that the Song is the script for a drama.

Murphy, Roland, O. Carm. *The Song of Songs.* HERM. Philadelphia: Fortress, 1990. This new, in-depth, technical, liberal commentary comes from a great scholar in wisdom literature. The fact that a Carmelite priest could do such a good analysis of a group of love poems is one more bit of evidence that exegetical skill is not the product of worldly experience.

Isaiah

Oswalt, John. *The Book of Isaiah, Chapters 1–39.* NICOT. Grand Rapids: Eerdmans, 1986. Oswalt's in-depth, technical, evangelical commentary takes Isaiah seriously in the best sense and is easily the best recent work on the first half of this biblical book.

Young, E. J. *The Book of Isaiah.* 3 vols. NICOT. Grand Rapids: Eerdmans, 1965–72. This in-depth, technical, evangelical commentary isn't easy reading; but Young was a giant of a scholar, and his commentary on Isaiah will not be outdated for a very long time.

Jeremiah

Holladay, William L. *Jeremiah 1.* (Chs. 1–25) HERM. Philadelphia: Fortress, 1986. *Jeremiah 2.* (Chs. 26–52) HERM. Philadelphia: Fortress, 1989. This in-depth, technical, liberal commentary is so thorough and thoughtful that I don't think it will be equaled for many years. Though Holladay is a liberal, his respect for the text is great, and evangelicals will surely profit greatly from these massive, masterful volumes.

Thompson, J. A. *The Book of Jeremiah.* NICOT. Grand Rapids: Eerdmans, 1980. This rather in-depth, technical commentary is also evangelical, and while lacking the detail of Holladay, still a judicious, sympathetic treatment of the prophecy.

Lamentations

Hillers, Delbert. *Lamentations.* AB. Garden City: Doubleday, 1973. Hiller's technical, liberal volume has no serious rival at the moment, in my opinion.

Ezekiel

Stuart, Douglas. *Ezekiel.* Communicator's Commentary (a series not otherwise included; see Preface). Dallas: Word Books, 1989. I wrote this to be a detailed, popular, evangelical commentary that would be the best in its category. Until someone else does a better job (which I would be glad to acknowledge) this remains my pick, especially because I take more care with the theology of this biblical book than do most commentators.

Zimmerli, Walther. *Ezekiel 1.* (Chs. 1–24); *Ezekiel 2.* (Chs. 25–48) HERM. Philadelphia: Fortress, 1979, 1983. This in-depth, technical, liberal volume from the Hermeneia is in fact one of the best in the series.

Daniel

Baldwin, Joyce. *Daniel.* TOTC. Downers Grove, IL: InterVarsity, 1978. This serious, evangelical volume is detailed, remarkably convincing, and especially helpful to the reader dealing with the difficult apocalyptic visions of the book.

Goldingay, John E. *Daniel.* WBC. Dallas: Word Books, 1989. A new, in-depth, technical, liberal book whose special strength is its format, something that makes all the volumes in the WBC series highly convenient to use.

Hosea

Mays, James. *Hosea, A Commentary.* OTL. Louisville: Westminster/John Knox, 1969. Among the liberal volumes on Hosea, this is the best, noteworthy for its real appreciation for the issues Hosea was addressing and his manner of doing so.

Stuart, Douglas. *Hosea–Jonah.* WBC. Waco, TX: Word Books, 1987. My own in-depth, technical, evangelical commentary treats Hosea as I think it must be understood—i.e., as a set of prophecies based squarely on the Mosaic covenant and not, as many commentators have assumed, as innovative, creative theology from a prophet whose wife cheated on him.

Joel

Wolff, Hans Walter. *Joel and Amos.* HERM. Philadelphia: Fortress, 1977. This in-depth, technical, liberal commentary is strong mainly in its comparative approach to Joel.

Stuart, Douglas. *Hosea–Jonah.* WBC. Waco, TX: Word Books, 1987. My fairly detailed, technical, evangelical treatment of Joel understands the book a bit more convincingly than others, I think, especially with regard to the identity of the army described in the bulk of the first two chapters.

Amos

Smith, Gary. *Amos: A Commentary.* Grand Rapids: Zondervan, 1989. Smith's in-depth, relatively technical, evangelical commentary is almost as good as mine in understanding Amos, and by reason of being somewhat more detailed deserves to be listed here.

Obadiah

Watts, John D. W. *Obadiah.* Grand Rapids: Eerdmans, 1969. Watts's is the only in-depth, technical, commentary on Obadiah that is self-contained. Therefore, in spite of its somewhat idiosyncratic views on some of the issues, this is the "authority" to consult.

Jonah

Stuart, Douglas. *Hosea–Jonah.* WBC. Waco, TX: Word Books, 1987. My in-depth, technical, evangelical commentary is one of the very few in existence that considers Jonah an historical book and argues the case for its historicity systematically.

Micah

Hillers, Delbert. *Micah.* HERM. Philadelphia: Fortress, 1983. Like other Hermeneia volumes, this one is in-depth, technical, and liberal. Hillers is a first-rate scholar, and he has a good feel for prophetic literature.

Nahum

Maier, Walter. *The Book of Nahum.* St. Louis: Concordia Publishing House, 1959. Repr. Grand Rapids: Baker Book House, 1980. This is just about the only in-depth, technical, evangelical commentary on Nahum, and also one of the very few high-quality commentaries on the book that is self-contained as a single volume.

Habakkuk

Armerding, Carl. *Habakkuk.* EBC. Grand Rapids: Zondervan, 1985. Armerding's detailed, serious, evangelical commentary on Habakkuk is hardly exhaustive in scope, but is sensible and clear. To buy it you must buy some other commentaries bound with it that you may not want as much, however.

Zephaniah

Baker, David. *Nahum, Habakkuk, Zephaniah.* TOTC. Downers Grove, IL: InterVarsity, 1989. This serious, evangelical volume also offers a decent treatment of Nahum and Habakkuk.

Haggai

Baldwin, Joyce. *Haggai, Zechariah, Malachi.* TOTC. Downers Grove, IL: InterVarsity, 1972. This is yet another of Baldwin's detailed, serious, evangelical TOTC commentaries that always do justice to the concerns of the inquiring student.

Verhoef, Pieter A. *The Books of Haggai and Malachi.* NICOT. Grand Rapids: Eerdmans, 1987. Verhoef's recent in-depth, technical, evangelical commentary had the advantage of being able to use Baldwin's (and many others') good work on these books.

Zechariah

Baldwin, Joyce. *Haggai, Zechariah, Malachi.* TOTC. Downers Grove, IL: InterVarsity, 1972. Baldwin's consistency and clarity mean that Zechariah, too, is highly accessible to the reader.

Malachi

Kaiser, Walter C., Jr. *Malachi: God's Unchanging Love.* Grand Rapids: Baker, 1984. A relatively in-depth, somewhat technical, evangelical commentary that genuinely understands what's going on in Malachi.

New Testament Commentaries

Matthew

Carson, Donald. *Matthew.* EBC. Grand Rapids: Zondervan, 1984. Much more in-depth, technical, and evangelical than its neighbors in the series volume, this work on Matthew is worth owning.

Hill, David. *The Gospel of Matthew.* Rev. ed. NCBC. Grand Rapids: Eerdmans, 1981. Hill's detailed, serious, liberal commentary is cautious, precise, clear, and very helpful to the reader who wants to understand Matthew well.

Mark

Lane, William L. *The Gospel of Mark.* NICNT. Grand Rapids: Eerdmans, 1973. Lane's in-depth, semi-technical, evangelical commentary has not yet been surpassed.

Luke

Danker, Frederick W. *Jesus and the New Age: A Commentary on St. Luke's Gospel.* Philadelphia: Fortress Press, 1988. Danker has written a detailed, serious, conservative-moderate commentary that will especially reward the reader who wants to understand Luke but doesn't know any Greek or a lot about NT research.

Marshall, I. Howard. *The Gospel of Luke: A Commentary on the Greek Text.* NIGTC. Grand Rapids: Eerdmans, 1978. Marshall's in-depth, technical, evangelical commentary has the special merit of explaining to the reader the full range of interpretational options for any given passage, but often you wish that Marshall himself would tell you more clearly where he actually stands on the options.

John

Brown, Raymond E. *The Gospel according to John.* 2 vols. AB. Garden City: Doubleday, 1966, 1970. In contrast to most of the AB volumes from the 1960s and 1970s, this one is in-depth, techni-cal, and conservative-moderate. Brown knows John so well that there are gems for the reader throughout.

Morris, Leon. *Reflections on the Gospel of John, Vol 1.* [John 1–5]. 1986. *Vol 2.* [John 6–10]. 1987. *Vol 3.* [John 11–16]. 1988. *Vol 4.* [John 17–21]. 1989. Grand Rapids: Baker. These four detailed, serious, evangelical volumes are the work of a senior scholar who homes in on the essentials in a most helpful way.

Acts

Bruce, F. F. *The Acts of the Apostles.* 3d ed., revised and enlarged. Grand Rapids: Eerdmans, 1989. Bruce's in-depth, technical, evan-gelical commentary on Acts is reflective of his renowned skill as a commentary writer. He has written a commentary on every book of the NT, and this is one of his best. It is certainly hard to beat among all commentaries written on the Book of Acts.

Marshall, I. Howard. *Acts.* TNTC. Grand Rapids: Eerdmans, 1980. Marshall is also a great commentator, and this commentary on Acts, detailed, serious, and evangelical, completes his coverage of Luke–Acts. The commentary is crystal clear, erudite through-out, compact without sacrificing quality, and alert to the issues that an interpreter want to be aware of.

Romans

Morris, Leon. *The Epistle to the Romans.* Downers Grove, Ill: Intervarsity, 1988. Morris's commentary is detailed, serious, and evangelical, and helps the reader through the grand theological expositions of the inspired apostle. It is not exactly miles ahead of the competition, but far enough ahead to be clearly a leader among the many written on Romans.

Cranfield, C. E. B. *Romans.* 2 vols. ICC. Edinburgh: T. & T. Clark, 1975, 1979. Cranfield contributes this volume to the new ICC, and like all the ICC volumes, new or old, it is in-depth, technical, and liberal. However, Romans is a book less likely to be ruined by a liberal commentator for an evangelical reader, so there is much to profit from here for evangelical and non-evangelical alike.

1 Corinthians

Fee, Gordon D. *1 Corinthians.* NICNT. Grand Rapids: Eerdmans, 1987. Fee put countless hours into this in-depth, technical, evangelical commentary, and I think it gives the reader more depth of careful analysis, more up-to-date insight, and more erudition on textual and linguistic matters than any other volume on this great letter of Paul's. Fee's expertise as a text critic solves more than one thorny problem in the book.

2 Corinthians

Furnish, Victor Paul. *2 Corinthians.* AB. Garden City: Doubleday, 1984. Furnish's volume is one of the later, in-depth, technical, liberal volumes in the AB series. It provides excellent coverage of the key issues and can be used profitably by persons of any theological persuasion.

Harris, Murray. *2 Corinthians.* EBC. Grand Rapids: Zondervan, 1976. A detailed, serious, evangelical commentary by one of the best evangelical NT scholars, far better in quality than most of the other EBC commentaries.

Galatians

Betz, Hans Dieter. *Galatians.* HERM. Philadelphia: Fortress, 1979. Betz is conservative-moderate in his approach to Galatians, and the commentary, like all in the Hermeneia series, is in-depth, technical, and strongly cognizant of comparative literature. Betz knows biblical theology well, and that is essential for accuracy in the study of Galatians, an often misinterpreted book.

Fung, Ronald Y. K. *The Epistle to the Galatians.* NICNT. Grand Rapids: Eerdmans, 1988. Fung's recent commentary is aware of the scholarly debates on Paul's view of the law, is detailed, serious, and evangelical, and contains many helpful observations useful to the preacher/teacher.

Ephesians

Barth, Markus. *Ephesians*. 2 vols. AB. Garden City: Doubleday, 1975. Ephesians hardly lacks for commentators, but this commentary from the mid-seventies is still the best overall. It is in-depth, technical, and liberal in theology, but not liberal in a way that would render it excessively offensive to an evangelical user.

Philippians

Hawthorne, Gerald. *Philippians*. WBC. Waco, TX: Word Books, 1983. Hawthorne's in-depth, technical commentary is evangelical, and in spite of being pedestrian at points is still one of the best available.

Martin, Ralph P. *The Epistle of Paul to the Philippians*. NCBC. Grand Rapids: Eerdmans, 1980. Martin is deservedly well known for this commentary, which is detailed, serious, and conservative-moderate. Martin has an enviable mastery over the scholarly literature, and he uses this knowledge to good advantage without seeming to show off to the reader or distract from careful analysis of the scriptural text.

Colossians

Bruce, F. F. *The Epistles to the Colossians, to Philemon, and to the Ephesians*. Rev. ed. NICNT. Grand Rapids: Eerdmans, 1984. Bruce has probably never written a bad commentary, and certainly this one, detailed, serious, and evangelical, is yet one more proof of his excellent expository skill.

O'Brien, Peter F. *Colossians, Philemon*. WBC. Waco, TX: Word Books, 1982. O'Brien's book is in many ways exemplary, and follows the WBC pattern in being in-depth, technical, and in this instance, also fully evangelical. It should be a standard for a long time to come.

1 and 2 Thessalonians

Bruce, F. F. *1 and 2 Thessalonians*. WBC. Waco, TX: Word Books, 1982. What is said about Bruce and O'Brien above could be said about Bruce here. His commentary, which is in-depth, technical, and evangelical, is just one more of his great contributions to NT scholarship. He is irenic to those he disagrees with, always helpful to the reader, and well informed on the issues and literature that a proper scholar should know.

Marshall, I. Howard. *1 and 2 Thessalonians.* NCBC. Grand
Rapids: Eerdmans, 1983. Like Bruce, Marshall is a gifted commentator, and this commentary, though not as detailed as that of
Bruce on these biblical books, is detailed, technically solid, and
evangelical. You can always follow the issues and be sure you know
the options for resolving them in a Marshall commentary.

1, 2 Timothy and Titus

Fee, Gordon. *1 and 2 Timothy, Titus.* GNC. San Francisco: Harper
and Row, 1984. Fee, Gordon. *1 and 2 Timothy, Titus.* NIC. [repr.
of above based on NIV rather than GNB]. Peabody, MA: Hendrickson, 1988. Fee's commentary is lengthy, technically first-rate
yet presented to the serious, non-specialist reader in a comprehensible way, and evangelical. He has wrestled with all the issues—and
there certainly are many of them in the Pastoral Epistles—and his
solutions to problems nearly always seem to me to be convincingly
presented

Kelly, J. N. D. *A Commentary on the Pastoral Epistles.* HNTC. New
York: Harper and Row, 1963; Repr. Grand Rapids: Baker, 1981
repr. Peabody, MA: Hendrickson, 1987. This detailed, technical,
conservative-moderate commentary is a sort of recent "classic"
commentary on the pastorals and it rightly deserves the reprintings
that have kept it in the eye of the public.

Philemon

Bruce, F. F. *The Epistles to the Colossians, to Philemon, and to the
Ephesians.* Rev. ed. NICNT. Grand Rapids: Eerdmans, 1984. Philemon is too short a book to have received its own self-contained commentaries very often, but this evangelical treatment includes the
best detailed, non-technical coverage of the book that I know of.

Martin, Ralph P. *Colossians and Philemon.* 3d ed. NCBC.
Grand Rapids: Eerdmans, 1981. Martin's semi-detailed, technical,
conservative-moderate commentary pays fully adequate attention
to Philemon in a judicious, careful exposition characteristic of all
Martin's work.

Hebrews

Bruce, F. F. *The Book of Hebrews.* NICNT. Grand Rapids: Eerdmans, 1964. He's written a lot of commentaries, and once again, one
of them is the best. This in-depth, somewhat technical, evangelical

commentary is a classic and deserves to be. Bruce's strong knowledge of the OT (he has written OT commentaries as well) has undoubtedly helped him especially with Hebrews.

James

Laws, Sophie. *A Commentary on the Epistle of James.* HNTC. New York: Harper and Row, 1980. Laws's commentary is detailed, serious, and liberal. It is not as long as Martin's but nevertheless covers the book remarkably carefully.

Martin, Ralph P. *James.* WBC. Waco, TX: Word Books, 1988. This relatively new commentary is in-depth, technical, conservative-moderate and, though not necessarily by a wide margin, the best longer work on James.

1 Peter

Kelly, J. N. D. *A Commentary on the Epistles of Peter and Jude.* HNTC. New York: Harper and Row, 1969. Kelly's detailed, technical, theologically conservative commentary is the best of the volumes covering both epistles of Peter.

Michaels, J. Ramsey. *1 Peter.* WBC. Waco, TX: Word Books, 1988. Michaels has produced a fine, in-depth, technical, conservative-moderate commentary that is recent enough to have the benefit of some scholarly work that Kelly and some other commentators simply did not have available to them. Michaels addresses the thorny issues of 1 Peter remarkably well, and solves some of them better than any other commentator, I think.

2 Peter

Green, Michael. *The Second Epistle General of Peter and the General Epistle of Jude.* Rev. ed. TNTC. Grand Rapids: Eerdmans, 1988. This is an up-to-date, detailed, serious, evangelical volume on Peter's tricky "last testament," and Green handles it well. He's a very skillful writer, and well aware of the battlegrounds one must encamp on when dealing with this epistle.

Kelly, J. N. D. *A Commentary on the Epistles of Peter and Jude.* HNTC. New York: Harper and Row, 1969. One-to-one, detailed, technical, conservative-moderate. See above.

1, 2, 3 John

Marshall, I. Howard. *The Epistles of John.* NICNT. Grand Rapids: Eerdmans, 1978. Another fine, in-depth, technical, evangelical commentary from someone who hardly seems able to fail at helping readers understand NT books.

Jude

Bauckham, Richard. *Jude, 2 Peter.* WBC. Waco, TX: Word Books, 1983. This relatively liberal commentary is in-depth in its coverage and technical, but usable by the non-specialist. It seems to me relatively better on Jude than on 2 Peter. Other commentaries now underway on these books will challenge Bauckham's preeminence, I predict.

Kelly, J. N. D. *A Commentary on the Epistles of Peter and Jude.* HNTC. New York: Harper and Row, 1969. A straightforward, careful, judicious, detailed, technical, conservative commentary on the complicated little epistle of Jude.

Revelation

Beasley-Murray, G. R. *The Book of Revelation.* Rev. ed. NCBC. Grand Rapids: Eerdmans, 1981. Revelation needs a lot of explaining, and this commentary does it better for the non-specialist than any other. It is not very lengthy, and not very technical, but a fine example of solid evangelical scholarship that is not likely to be outdated for a long time to come.

Mounce, Robert H. *The Book of Revelation.* NICNT. Grand Rapids: Eerdmans, 1977. Mounce's longer commentary on the Bible's closing book is fairly technical and evangelical, and a judicious, balanced work on a book so often abused and misunderstood that one wishes everyone could have a chance to read this kind of commentary on it.

Appendix 1:
A Brief List of Definitions

Commentary: A passage-by-passage explanation of the content of all or part of the Bible. The word *commentary* is used to indicate both individual commentaries on individual books of the Bible, and a collection of many individual commentaries combined together. ("Commentaries" on the Bible have within them "commentaries" on each of the books.) See Preface and chapters 1 and 2.

Commentator: The writer of a commentary.

Critical commentary: A commentary volume or series that analyzes the text in depth and pays close attention to problems of any sort.

Editor: The scholar chosen by a publisher to supervise the writing and production of a commentary/commentaries, including securing authors for individual volumes and rewriting some of their material, if necessary.

Epistles: Letters in the New Testament, such as Romans, Galatians, etc.

Exegesis: The close, careful, analytical study of a passage (usually in the original language) with the aim of understanding with full accuracy its meaning.

Exegetical: Based on or paying ample attention to proper exegesis.

Hermeneutical: Interpretational. Hermeneutics is the science of interpretation.

Passage: A section of a biblical book devoted to a particular topic or sub-topic.

Pentateuch: The first five books of the Old Testament.

Pericope: A passage. *Pericope* is often used instead of passage to emphasize the fact that the beginning and end points of the passage are clearly delineated so that it may be treated as a unitary piece of Scripture rather than only as part of a greater whole.

Series: A group of commentaries on various biblical books published as separate volumes over a period of time—eventually, if completed, forming a complete set.

Set: All the commentary volumes published in a series.

Volume: A self-contained, bound book containing commentary on any number of biblical books. Many volumes make a series, or a set.

Appendix 2: Abbreviations

AB	The Anchor Bible. Garden City: Doubleday.
ACNT	Augsburg Commentary on the New Testament. Minneapolis: Augsburg (now Augsburg Fortress).
BSC	The Bible Study Commentary. Grand Rapids: Zondervan (Lamplighter Books).
CBCNEB	The Cambridge Bible Commentary on the New English Bible. New York and Cambridge: Cambridge University Press.
CC	Continental Commentaries. Minneapolis: Augsburg (now Augsburg Fortress).
DSB	The Daily Study Bible. Philadelphia: Westminster Press.
ed.	edition
Ed.	Editor; Edited by
EBC	Expositor's Bible Commentary. Grand Rapids: Zondervan.
GNB	Good News Bible, also known as Today's English Version. Published by the American Bible Society, 1976.
GNC	Good News Commentaries. San Francisco: Harper and Row.
HERM	Hermeneia: A Critical and Historical Commentary on the Bible. Philadelphia: Fortress Press.
HNTC	Harper's New Testament Commentaries. New York: Harper and Row.
IB	Interpreter's Bible. Nashville: Abingdon Press.
ICC	The International Critical Commentary. Edinburgh: T. & T. Clark [and a number of other publishers in the U.S. for various volumes].
INT	Interpretation: A Bible Commentary for Teaching and Preaching. Atlanta: John Knox [now Louisville: Westminster/John Knox].
ITC	International Theological Commentary. Grand Rapids: Eerdmans.
K-D	Keil and Delitzsch. C. F. Keil and F. Delitzsch, Biblical Commentary on the Old Testament. Repr. Grand Rapids: Eerdmans.
LBC	Layman's Bible Commentary. Atlanta: John Knox.
NCBC	New Century Bible Commentary. Grand Rapids: Eerdmans; London: Marshall, Morgan and Scott.

NIBC	New International Bible Commentary. Peabody, MA: Hendrickson Publishers.
NICNT	New International Commentary on the New Testament. Grand Rapids: Eerdmans.
NICOT	New International Commentary on the Old Testament. Grand Rapids: Eerdmans.
NIGTC	New International Greek Testament Commentary. Grand Rapids: Eerdmans.
NIV	New International Version of the Bible. Published by Zondervan; copyright 1984, International Bible Society.
NT	New Testament
NTC	New Testament Commentaries. Philadelphia: Trinity Press International.
NTM	New Testament Message. A Biblical-Theological Commentary. Wilmington, DE: Michael Glazier.
OT	Old Testament
OTL	The Old Testament Library. Philadelphia: Westminster Press.
OTM	Old Testament Message. A Biblical-Theological Commentary. Wilmington, DE: Michael Glazier.
PC	Proclamation Commentaries. The Old Testament Witness for Preaching. Philadelphia: Fortress Press.
Repr.	Reprint
RSV	Revised Standard Version
TAI	Text and Interpretation. A Practical Commentary. Grand Rapids: Eerdmans.
TBC	Torch Bible Commentary. London: SCM.
TBST	The Bible Speaks Today. Leicester, England; Downers Grove, IL: InterVarsity.
TNTC	Tyndale New Testament Commentaries. Grand Rapids: Eerdmans [latest volumes Downers Grove, IL: InterVarsity].
TOTC	Tyndale Old Testament Commentaries. Grand Rapids: Eerdmans [latest volumes Downers Grove, IL: InterVarsity].
WBC	Word Biblical Commentary. Dallas: Word Books.

Douglas Stuart is chair of the Division of Biblical Studies at Gordon-Conwell Theological Seminary in Massachusetts, and also Senior Pastor of First Church Congregational of Boxford, Massachusetts. He holds the B.A. and Ph.D. degrees from Harvard, and has contributed volumes to several commentary series.